MW00948006

The Innovative
Ninja CREAMI Cookbook 2023

1600 Days of Low-Sugar, Low-Fat, and High-Quality Ninja CREAMI Recipes for Beginners and Pros Alike, Ideal for Summer BBQs and Birthday Parties

Darlene M. Garcia

Copyright © 2023 by Darlene M. Garcia- All rights reserved.

The content contained within this book may not be reproduced, duplicated, or transmitted without direct written permission from the author or the publisher. Under no circumstances will any blame or legal responsibility be held against the publisher, or author, for any damages, reparation, or monetary loss due to the information contained within this book, either directly or indirectly.

Legal Notice: This book is copyright protected. It is only for personal use. You cannot amend, distribute, sell, use, quote or paraphrase any part, or the content within this book, without the consent of the author or publisher.

Disclaimer Notice: Please note the information contained within this document is for educational and entertainment purposes only. All effort has been executed to present accurate, up to date, reliable, complete information. No warranties of any kind are declared or implied. Readers acknowledge that the author is not engaged in the rendering of legal, financial, medical, or professional advice. The content within this book has been derived from various sources. Please consult a licensed professional before attempting any techniques outlined in this book. By reading this document, the reader agrees that under no circumstances is the author responsible for any losses, direct or indirect, that are incurred as a result of the use of the information contained within this document, including, but not limited to, errors, omissions, or inaccuracies.

CONTENTS

Smoothie Bowls Recipes 35

Ice Cream Mix-ins Recipes 46

Milkshake Recipes 59

Gelato Recipes 68

Introduction

Introducing "Ninja CREAMi Cookbook" – the culmination of my passion for cooking and creating delicious frozen desserts with the Ninja CREAMi Ice Cream Maker. This cookbook contains over 1600 unique and creative recipes that will take your dessert game to the next level.

My name is Darlene M. Garcia, and I've been using the Ninja CREAMi Ice Cream Maker for over 1000 days now. During that time, I've experimented with countless recipes and flavors, and I've learned a lot about how to get the most out of this amazing appliance. As a busy working mom, I know how important it is to have quick and easy dessert options that don't require a lot of fuss or preparation. That's why I created this cookbook – to share my favorite recipes and tips with others who love to cook and create.

I believe that food brings people together and can be a source of joy and comfort in our lives. And with the Ninja CREAMi Ice Cream Maker, creating delicious and unique frozen desserts has never been easier. I wanted to show people how versatile and fun this appliance can be, and inspire them to try new flavors and techniques.

First and foremost, you'll find over 100 delicious and creative recipes for ice cream, gelato, sorbet, and more. From classic flavors like vanilla and chocolate, to more exotic options like matcha and rose, there's something for every taste and preference. But this cookbook is more than just a collection of recipes. It's also packed with tips and tricks for getting the most out of your Ninja CREAMi Ice Cream Maker. You'll learn how to prevent ice crystals from forming, how to create creamy and smooth textures, and how to experiment with different mix-ins and toppings.

This Ninja CREAMi Cookbook is a labor of love that I hope will inspire others to cook and create delicious frozen desserts with their Ninja CREAMi Ice Cream Maker. Whether you're a beginner or an experienced cook, there's something in this cookbook for everyone. So why not give it a try and see what delicious creations you can come up with?

What is Ninja Creami?

Ninja Creami is a kitchen appliance that allows users to quickly and easily prepare a variety of frozen treats in the comfort of their own home. This innovative device is designed to create ice cream, sorbet, and gelato using a unique freezing system that eliminates the need for pre-freezing or ice.

Additionally, the device comes with a variety of accessories, such as a paddle, measuring cup, and storage containers, to ensure that users have everything they need to create delicious frozen treats.

Using the Ninja Creami is incredibly simple and straightforward. To make a batch of ice cream, for example, users need only add the required ingredients to the device and press a button. The machine does all the work, and within minutes, users can enjoy their own homemade ice cream.

One of the key features of the Ninja Creami is its compact size and portability. Unlike traditional ice cream makers, which can be bulky and difficult to store, the Ninja Creami is small enough to fit on a kitchen counter or table and can be easily packed up and taken on the go.

It's important to note that the Ninja Creami uses both electricity and liquefied gas, so users should be sure to carefully read the instruction manual and safety guidelines before operating the device.

How Ninja Creami works?

The Ninja Creami uses a unique freezing system to create a variety of frozen treats, such as ice cream, sorbet, and gelato. The device is designed to be quick and easy to use, and it eliminates the need for pre-freezing or using ice, making it a convenient option for anyone who loves frozen desserts.

The Ninja Creami's freezing system combines a mixture of liquefied gas and liquid ingredients to freeze the mixture in the mixer bowl. To use the device, users simply add the ingredients for their chosen recipe to the mixer bowl, and then add the recommended amount of liquefied gas through a small opening in the lid. The mixer bowl is then placed in the machine, and the device begins to freeze the mixture while mixing it with a paddle.

The Ninja Creami's freezing system is designed to create a smooth and creamy texture, similar to traditional ice cream or gelato. The paddle helps to mix the ingredients evenly, ensuring that the mixture freezes evenly and doesn't become too icy or grainy. The machine's built-in timer and automatic shut-off feature ensure that the mixture is frozen and mixed for the right amount of time, helping to prevent over-churning and ensuring a perfect consistency every time.

In addition to the mixer bowl and lid, the Ninja Creami comes with a variety of accessories to help users create their own custom frozen treats. These include a paddle, measuring cup, and storage containers. The paddle is used to mix the ingredients in the mixer bowl and create a smooth and creamy texture. The measuring cup helps users measure out the ingredients for each recipe, ensuring that they get the right proportions for their frozen treats. The storage containers are used to store the finished product, and they come with air-tight lids to keep the treats fresh and prevent freezer burn.

The machine should be used in a well-ventilated area and should not be left unattended during operation. Additionally, users should be aware of the ingredients used in each recipe and choose accordingly, as many of the recipes call for dairy or other common allergens.

The Ninja Creami is a versatile and convenient kitchen appliance that allows users to create delicious frozen treats in just a matter of minutes. Its unique freezing system, recipe book, and accessories make it a great option for anyone who loves frozen desserts and wants to make their own custom creations at home.

How Ninja Creami is different from traditional ice cream machines?

● **Freezing System**

One of the key differences between the Ninja Creami and traditional ice cream machines is its freezing system. The Ninja Creami uses a proprietary freezing system that combines a mixture of liquefied gas and liquid ingredients to freeze the mixture in the mixer bowl. Unlike other ice cream machines that require pre-freezing the bowl or adding ice, the Ninja Creami's freezing system is designed to be quick and efficient, allowing users to make frozen treats in just a matter of minutes.

● **Operation**

Using the Ninja Creami is simple and straightforward. To make a batch of ice cream, for example, users need to add the required ingredients to the mixer bowl and press a button. The machine will then freeze and mix the ingredients, creating a smooth and creamy texture. Traditional ice cream machines may require additional steps, such as pre-freezing the bowl or mixing the ingredients manually, which can make the process more time-consuming and complicated.

● **Size and Portability**

Another difference between the Ninja Creami and traditional ice cream machines is its size and portability. The Ninja Creami is designed to be compact and easy to store, unlike traditional ice cream machines, which can be bulky and difficult to store. The Ninja Creami is also easy to transport, so users can take it with them to picnics, parties, or other events where they want to serve homemade frozen treats.

The benefits of using Ninja Creami

● **Convenience**

One of the main benefits of using the Ninja Creami is its convenience. Unlike traditional ice cream machines, the Ninja Creami does not require pre-freezing or using ice. This means that users can make delicious frozen treats in just a matter of minutes, without having to wait for the bowl to freeze or worry about running out of ice. The Ninja Creami is also easy to clean and store, making it a convenient appliance for everyday use.

● **Customization**

Another benefit of using the Ninja Creami is the ability to customize the recipes to suit individual preferences. Users can experiment with different flavors and ingredients to create their own custom frozen treats.

- **Texture**

The Ninja Creami's unique freezing system and mixer bowl and paddle are designed to create a smooth and creamy texture for frozen treats. This means that users can enjoy delicious and creamy ice cream, sorbet, and gelato without the grainy or icy texture that can sometimes result from using traditional ice cream machines. The Ninja Creami's built-in timer and automatic shut-off feature also ensure that the mixture is frozen and mixed for the right amount of time, helping to prevent over-churning and ensuring a perfect texture every time.

- **Affordability**

Compared to other kitchen appliances, the Ninja Creami is relatively affordable, making it a great investment for anyone who loves frozen treats. The device is also built to last, with a durable design and high-quality materials. This means that users can enjoy their favorite frozen treats for years to come, without having to worry about replacing the appliance.

- **Health Benefits**

Another benefit of using the Ninja Creami is the ability to create healthier frozen treats at home. Users can experiment with different ingredients and reduce the amount of sugar and fat in their recipes, creating treats that are lower in calories and fat than store-bought options. The device also allows users to control the quality and freshness of the ingredients, ensuring that they are using high-quality and natural ingredients in their recipes.

- **Portability**

The Ninja Creami is designed to be compact and portable, making it a great option for anyone who wants to take their frozen treats on-the-go. Users can take the device to picnics, parties, or other events where they want to serve homemade frozen treats. The device is also easy to store, making it a convenient appliance for small kitchens or apartments.

In conclusion, the Ninja Creami is a versatile and convenient kitchen appliance that offers several benefits for anyone who loves frozen treats. Its convenience, customization, texture, affordability, health benefits, and portability make it a great investment for anyone who wants to create delicious and creamy frozen treats at home or on-the-go. By following the instructions and safety guidelines, users can enjoy their favorite frozen treats in just a matter of minutes, without having to worry about pre-freezing or using ice.

Ice Cream Recipes

Matcha Ice Cream

Servings: 4
Cooking Time: 10 Seconds
Ingredients:

- 1 tablespoon cream cheese, softened
- ⅓ cup granulated sugar
- 2 tablespoons matcha powder
- 1 teaspoon vanilla extract
- 1 cup whole milk
- ¾ cup heavy cream

Directions:

1. In a large microwave-safe bowl, add the cream cheese and microwave for on High for about ten seconds.
2. Remove from the microwave and stir until smooth.
3. Add the sugar, matcha powder and vanilla extract and with a wire whisk, beat until the mixture looks like frosting.
4. Slowly add the milk and heavy cream and beat until well combined.
5. Transfer the mixture into an empty Ninja CREAMi pint container.
6. Cover the container with storage lid and freeze for 24 hours.
7. After 24 hours, remove the lid from container and arrange into the Outer Bowl of Ninja CREAMi.
8. Install the Creamerizer Paddle onto the lid of Outer Bowl.
9. Then rotate the lid clockwise to lock.
10. Press Power button to turn on the unit.
11. Then press Ice Cream button.
12. When the program is completed, turn the Outer Bowl and release it from the machine.
13. Transfer the ice cream into serving bowls and serve immediately.

Nutrition Info:

- InfoCalories: 188,Fat: 11.2g,Carbohydrates: 20.3g,Protein: 2.6.

Strawberry-carrot Ice Cream

Servings:4
Cooking Time:x
Ingredients:

- 1 cup frozen carrot slices, thawed
- ½ cup trimmed and quartered fresh strawberries
- 1 tablespoon cream cheese, at room temperature
- ⅓ cup granulated sugar
- 1 teaspoon strawberry extract
- ½ cup whole milk
- 5 drops red food coloring
- ½ cup heavy (whipping) cream

Directions:

1. Combine the carrots, strawberries, cream cheese, sugar, strawberry extract, milk, and food coloring in a blender. Blend on high until smooth.
2. Pour the base into a clean CREAMi Pint. Whisk in the heavy cream until combined. Place the storage lid on the container and freeze for 24 hours.
3. Remove the CREAMi Pint from the freezer and take off the lid. Place the pint in the outer bowl of your Ninja CREAMi, install the Creamerizer Paddle in the outer bowl lid, and lock the lid assembly onto the outer bowl. Place the bowl assembly on the motor base, and twist the handle to the right to raise the platform and lock it in place. Select the Ice Cream function.
4. Once the machine has finished processing, remove the ice cream from the pint. Serve immediately with desired toppings.

Chocolate & Spinach Ice Cream

Servings: 2
Cooking Time:x
Ingredients:

- ½ C. frozen spinach, thawed and squeezed dry
- 1 C. whole milk
- ½ C. granulated sugar
- 1 tsp. mint extract
- 3-5 drops green food coloring
- 1/3 C. heavy cream
- ¼ C. chocolate chunks, chopped
- ¼ C. brownie, cut into 1-inch pieces

Directions:

1. In a high-speed blender, add the spinach, milk, sugar, mint extract and food coloring and pulse until mixture smooth.
2. Transfer the mixture into an empty Ninja CREAMi pint container.
3. Add the heavy cream and stir until well combined.
4. Cover the container with the storage lid and freeze for 24 hours.
5. After 24 hours, remove the lid from container and arrange into the outer bowl of Ninja CREAMi.
6. Install the "Creamerizer Paddle" onto the lid of outer bowl
7. Then rotate the lid clockwise to lock.
8. Press "Power" button to turn on the unit.
9. Then press "ICE CREAM" button.
10. When the program is completed, with a spoon, create a 1½-inch wide hole in the center that reaches the bottom of the pint container.
11. Add the chocolate chunks and brownie pieces into the hole and press "MIX-IN" button.
12. When the program is completed, turn the outer bowl and release it from the machine.
13. Transfer the ice cream into serving bowls and serve immediately.

Nutrition Info:

- InfoCalories: 243,Carbohydrates: 36.7g,Protein: 3.4g,Fat: 10.1g,Sodium: 55m.

Strawberry Ice Cream

Servings: 4
Cooking Time:x
Ingredients:

- ¼ cup sugar
- 1 tablespoon cream cheese, softened
- 1 teaspoon vanilla bean paste
- 1 cup milk
- ¾ cup heavy whipping cream
- 6 medium fresh strawberries, hulled and quartered

Directions:

1. In a bowl, add the sugar, cream cheese, vanilla bean paste and with a wire whisk, mix until well combined.
2. Add in the milk and heavy whipping cream and beat until well combined.
3. Transfer the mixture into an empty Ninja CREAMi pint container.
4. Add the strawberry pieces and stir to combine.
5. Cover the container with storage lid and freeze for 24 hours.
6. After 24 hours, remove the lid from container and arrange into the Outer Bowl of Ninja CREAMi.
7. Install the Creamerizer Paddle onto the lid of Outer Bowl.
8. Then rotate the lid clockwise to lock.
9. Press Power button to turn on the unit.
10. Then press Ice Cream button.
11. When the program is completed, turn the Outer Bowl and release it from the machine.
12. Transfer the ice cream into serving bowls and serve immediately.

Nutrition Info:

- InfoCalories: 175,Fat: 10.5g,Carbohydrates: 18.8g,Protein: 2.8.

Low-sugar Vanilla Ice Cream

Servings:4
Cooking Time:x
Ingredients:
- 1¾ cup fat-free half-and-half
- ¼ cup stevia cane sugar blend
- 1 teaspoon vanilla extract

Directions:
1. In a medium bowl, whisk the half-and-half, sugar, and vanilla together until everything is combined and the sugar is dissolved. The mixture will be foamy. Let it sit for 5 minutes or until the foam subsides.
2. Pour the base into a clean CREAMi Pint. Place the storage lid on the container and freeze for 24 hours.
3. Remove the CREAMi Pint from the freezer and take off the lid. Place the pint in the outer bowl of your Ninja CREAMi, install the Creamerizer Paddle in the outer bowl lid, and lock the lid assembly onto the outer bowl. Place the bowl assembly on the motor base, and twist the handle to the right to raise the platform and lock it in place. Select the Lite Ice Cream function.
4. Once the machine has finished processing, remove the ice cream from the pint. Serve immediately.

Lemon & Vanilla Ice Cream

Servings: 4
Cooking Time:x
Ingredients:
- 1 can full-fat unsweetened coconut milk
- ½ C. granulated sugar
- 1 tsp. vanilla extract
- 1 tsp. lemon extract

Directions:
1. In a bowl, add the coconut milk and beat until smooth.
2. Add the remaining ingredients and beat until well combined.
3. Transfer the mixture into an empty Ninja CREAMi pint container.
4. Cover the container with the storage lid and freeze for 24 hours.
5. After 24 hours, remove the lid from container and arrange into the outer bowl of Ninja CREAMi.
6. Install the "Creamerizer Paddle" onto the lid of outer bowl.
7. Then rotate the lid clockwise to lock.
8. Press "Power" button to turn on the unit.
9. Then press "ICE CREAM" button.
10. When the program is completed, turn the outer bowl and release it from the machine.
11. Transfer the ice cream into serving bowls and serve immediately.

Nutrition Info:
- InfoCalories: 280,Carbohydrates: 28.2g,Protein: 1.5g,Fat: 18.3g,Sodium: 23m.

Classic Vanilla Ice Cream

Servings:4
Cooking Time:x
Ingredients:

- 1 tablespoon cream cheese, at room temperature
- ⅓ cup granulated sugar
- 1 teaspoon vanilla extract
- ¾ cup heavy (whipping) cream
- 1 cup whole milk
- ¼ cup mini chocolate chips (optional)

Directions:

1. In a large microwave-safe bowl, add the cream cheese and microwave for 10 seconds. Add the sugar and vanilla extract, and with a whisk or rubber spatula, combine the mixture until it looks like frosting, about 60 seconds.
2. Slowly whisk in the heavy cream and milk and mix until the sugar is completely dissolved and the cream cheese is completely incorporated.
3. Pour the base into a clean CREAMi Pint. Place the storage lid on the container and freeze for 24 hours.
4. Remove the CREAMi Pint from the freezer and take off the lid. Place the pint container in the outer bowl of your Ninja CREAMi, install the Creamerizer Paddle in the outer bowl lid, and lock the lid assembly onto the outer bowl. Place the bowl assembly on the motor base, and twist the handle to the right to raise the platform and lock it in place. Select the Ice Cream function.
5. Once the machine has finished processing, remove the lid from the pint container. If you are adding chocolate chips: with a spoon, create a 1½-inch-wide hole that reaches the bottom of the pint. During this process, it is okay if your treat reaches above the Max Fill line. Add ¼ cup of mini chocolate chips to the hole in the pint, replace the lid, and select the Mix-In function.
6. Serve immediately with desired toppings.

Peanut Butter & Jelly Ice Cream

Servings: 4
Cooking Time: 5 Minutes
Ingredients:

- 3 tbsp. granulated sugar
- 4 large egg yolks
- 1 C. whole milk
- 1/3 C. heavy cream
- ¼ C. smooth peanut butter
- 3 tbsp. grape jelly
- ¼ C. honey roasted peanuts, chopped

Directions:

1. In a small saucepan, add the sugar and egg yolks and beat until well combined.
2. Add the milk, heavy cream, peanut butter, and grape jelly to the saucepan and stir to combine.
3. Place saucepan over medium heat and for about 3-5 minutes, stirring continuously.
4. Remove from the heat and through a fine-mesh strainer, strain the mixture into an empty Ninja CREAMi pint container.
5. Place the container into an ice bath to cool.
6. After cooling, cover the container with the storage lid and freeze for 24 hours.
7. After 24 hours, remove the lid from container and arrange into the outer bowl of Ninja CREAMi.
8. Install the "Creamerizer Paddle" onto the lid of outer bowl.
9. Then rotate the lid clockwise to lock.
10. Press "Power" button to turn on the unit.
11. Then press "ICE CREAM" button.
12. When the program is completed, with a spoon, create a 1½-inch wide hole in the center that reaches the bottom of the pint container.
13. Add the peanuts into the hole and press "MIX-IN" button.
14. When the program is completed, turn the outer bowl and release it from the machine.
15. Transfer the ice cream into serving bowls and serve immediately.

Nutrition Info:

- InfoCalories: 349,Carbohydrates: 27.5g,Protein: 11.5g,Fat: 23.1g,Sodium: 94m.

Cherry-chocolate Chunk Ice Cream

Servings: 4
Cooking Time: 24 Hours And 10minutes
Ingredients:

- 1 packet frozen sweet cherries
- ¾ cup heavy cream
- 1 can sweetened condensed milk
- ½ cup milk
- 1 teaspoon vanilla extract
- 1 bar semisweet baking chocolate, broken into small chunks

Directions:
1. Combine the heavy cream, sweetened condensed milk, milk, and vanilla extract in a mixing bowl.
2. Pour the ice cream mixture into an empty ninja CREAMi Pint container, add the chopped cherries and chocolate chunks, and freeze for 24 hours.
3. After 24 hours, remove the Pint from the freezer. Remove the lid.
4. Place the Ninja CREAMi Pint into the outer bowl. Place the outer bowl with the Pint in it into the ninja CREAMi machine and turn until the outer bowl locks into place. Push the ICE CREAM button.
5. Once the ICE CREAM function has ended, turn the outer bowl and release it from the ninja CREAMi machine.

Nutrition Info:

- InfoCalories 458,Protein 7.2g,Carbohydrate 48g,Fat 28g,Sodium 92mg.

Kale'd By Chocolate Ice Cream

Servings:4
Cooking Time:x
Ingredients:

- 1 cup frozen kale
- 1 tablespoon cream cheese, at room temperature
- ⅓ cup granulated sugar
- 3 tablespoons dark unsweetened cocoa powder
- ¾ cup whole milk
- ¾ cup heavy (whipping) cream

Directions:
1. Combine the frozen kale, cream cheese, sugar, cocoa powder, and milk in a blender. Blend on high until smooth.
2. Pour the base into a clean CREAMi Pint. Whisk in the heavy cream until combined. Place the storage lid on the container and freeze for 24 hours.
3. Remove the CREAMi Pint from the freezer and take off the lid. Place the pint in the outer bowl of your Ninja CREAMi, install the Creamerizer Paddle in outer bowl lid, and lock the lid assembly onto the outer bowl. Place the bowl assembly on the motor base, and twist the handle to the right to raise the platform and lock it in place. Select the Ice Cream function.
4. Once the machine has finished processing, remove the ice cream from the pint. Serve immediately with desired toppings.

'pea'nut Butter Ice Cream

Servings:4
Cooking Time:x
Ingredients:

- ½ cup frozen peas, thawed
- ½ cup plus 1 tablespoon granulated sugar
- 1 tablespoon corn syrup
- 2 tablespoons powdered peanut butter
- 1 cup whole milk
- 1 teaspoon vanilla extract
- ⅓ cup heavy (whipping) cream

Directions:
1. Combine the peas, sugar, corn syrup, powdered peanut butter, milk, and vanilla in a blender. Blend on high until smooth.
2. Pour the base into a clean CREAMi Pint. Whisk in the heavy cream until combined. Place the storage lid on the container and freeze for 24 hours.
3. Remove the CREAMi Pint from the freezer and take off the lid. Place the pint in outer bowl of your Ninja CREAMi, install the Creamerizer Paddle in the outer bowl lid, and lock the lid assembly onto the outer bowl. Place the bowl assembly on the motor base, and twist the handle to the right to raise the platform and lock it in place. Select the Ice Cream function.
4. Once the machine has finished processing, remove the ice cream from the pint. Serve immediately.

Coconut Ice Cream

Servings: 4

Cooking Time: 24 Hours And 5 Minutes

Ingredients:

- ½ cup milk
- 1 can cream of coconut
- ¾ cup heavy cream
- ½ cup sweetened flaked coconut

Directions:

1. In a food processor or blender, combine the milk and coconut cream and thoroughly mix.
2. Combine the heavy cream and flaked coconut in a mixing bowl, and then add to the milk-cream mixture. Combine well.
3. Pour the mixture into an empty ninja CREAMi Pint container and freeze for 24 hours.
4. After 24 hours, remove the Pint from the freezer. Remove the lid.
5. Place the Ninja CREAMi Pint into the outer bowl. Place the outer bowl with the Pint in it into the ninja CREAMi machine and turn until the outer bowl locks into place. Push the ICE CREAM button.
6. Once the ICE CREAM function has ended, turn the outer bowl and release it from the ninja CREAMi machine.

Nutrition Info:

- InfoCalories 406,Protein 3g,Carbohydrate 36g,Fat 29g,Sodium 86mg.

Earl Grey Tea Ice Cream

Servings: 4

Cooking Time: 25 Minutes

Ingredients:

- 1 cup heavy cream
- 1 cup whole milk
- 5 tablespoons monk fruit sweetener
- 3 Earl Grey tea bags

Directions:

1. In a medium saucepan, add cream and milk and stir to combine.
2. Place saucepan over medium heat and cook until for bout two-three minutes or until steam is rising.
3. Stir in the monk fruit sweetener and reduce the heat to very low.
4. Add teabags and cover the saucepan for about 20 minutes.
5. Discard the tea bags and remove saucepan from heat.
6. Transfer the mixture into an empty Ninja CREAMi pint container and place into an ice bath to cool.
7. After cooling, cover the container with storage lid and freeze for 24 hours.
8. After 24 hours, remove the lid from container and arrange into the Outer Bowl of Ninja CREAMi.
9. Install the Creamerizer Paddle onto the lid of Outer Bowl.
10. Then rotate the lid clockwise to lock.
11. Press Power button to turn on the unit.
12. Then press Ice Cream button.
13. When the program is completed, turn the Outer Bowl and release it from the machine.
14. Transfer the ice cream into serving bowls and serve immediately.

Nutrition Info:

- InfoCalories: 140,Fat: 13.1g,Carbohydrates: 3.6g,Protein: 2.6.

Mango Ice Cream

Servings: 1
Cooking Time: 24 Hours And 5 Minutes
Ingredients:
- 1 mango (medium-sized, cut into quarters)
- 1 tablespoon cream cheese (room temperature)
- ¼ cup sugar
- ¾ cup heavy whipping cream
- 1 cup milk

Directions:
1. Combine the cream cheese, sugar in a mixing bowl. Using a whisk, mix together until all ingredients are thoroughly combined, and the sugar starts to dissolve.
2. Add in the heavy whipping cream and milk. Whisk until all ingredients have combined well.
3. Pour mixture into an empty ninja CREAMi Pint container. Freeze for 24 hours after adding the mango to the Pint, ensuring you don't go over the maximum fill line.
4. Take the Pint out of the freezer after 24 hours. Take off the cover.
5. Place the Ninja CREAMi Pint into the outer bowl. Place the outer bowl with the Pint in it into the ninja CREAMi machine and turn until the outer bowl locks into place. Push the ICE CREAM button. During the ICE CREAM function, the ice cream will mix and become very creamy.
6. Once the ICE CREAM function has ended, turn the outer bowl and release it from the ninja CREAMi machine.

Nutrition Info:
- InfoCalories 96,Protein 6g,Carbohydrate 18g,Fat 0.1g,Sodium 156mg.

Pear Ice Cream

Servings: 4
Cooking Time: 15 Minutes
Ingredients:
- 3 medium ripe pears, peeled, cored and cut into 1-inch pieces
- 1 can full-fat unsweetened coconut milk
- ½ cup granulated sugar

Directions:
1. In a medium saucepan, add all ingredients and stir to combine.
2. Place the saucepan over medium heat and bring to a boil.
3. Reduce the heat to low and simmer for about ten minutes or until liquid is reduced by half.
4. Remove from the heat and set aside to cool.
5. After cooling, transfer the mixture into a high-speed blender and pulse until smooth.
6. Transfer the mixture into an empty Ninja CREAMi pint container.
7. Cover the container with storage lid and freeze for 24 hours.
8. After 24 hours, remove the lid from container and arrange into the Outer Bowl of Ninja CREAMi.
9. Install the Creamerizer Paddle onto the lid of Outer Bowl.
10. Then rotate the lid clockwise to lock.
11. Press Power button to turn on the unit.
12. Then press Ice Cream button.
13. When the program is completed, turn the Outer Bowl and release it from the machine.
14. Transfer the ice cream into serving bowls and serve immediately.

Nutrition Info:
- InfoCalories: 368,Fat: 18.5g,Carbohydrates: 51.9g,Protein: 2.1.

Mint Cookie Ice Cream

Servings: 4
Cooking Time:x
Ingredients:

- ¾ C. coconut cream
- ¼ C. monk fruit sweetener with Erythritol
- 2 tbsp. agave nectar
- ½ tsp. mint extract
- 5-6 drops green food coloring
- 1 C. oat milk
- 3 chocolate sandwich cookies, quartered

Directions:

1. In a large bowl, add the coconut cream and beat until smooth.
2. Add the sweetener, agave nectar, mint extract and food coloring and beat until sweetener is dissolved.
3. Add the oat milk and beat until well combined.
4. Transfer the mixture into an empty Ninja CREAMi pint container.
5. Cover the container with the storage lid and freeze for 24 hours.
6. After 24 hours, remove the lid from container and arrange into the outer bowl of Ninja CREAMi.
7. Install the "Creamerizer Paddle" onto the lid of outer bowl.
8. Then rotate the lid clockwise to lock.
9. Press "Power" button to turn on the unit.
10. Then press "LITE ICE CREAM" button.
11. When the program is completed, with a spoon, create a 1½-inch wide hole in the center that reaches the bottom of the pint container.
12. Add the cookie pieces into the hole and press "MIX-IN" button.
13. When the program is completed, turn the outer bowl and release it from the machine.
14. Transfer the ice cream into serving bowls and serve immediately.

Nutrition Info:

- InfoCalories: 201,Carbohydrates: 21.9g,Protein: 2.4g,Fat: 12.8g,Sodium: 69m.

Lemon Ice Cream

Servings: 4
Cooking Time:x
Ingredients:

- 1 can full-fat unsweetened coconut milk
- ½ cup granulated sugar
- 1 teaspoon vanilla extract
- 1 teaspoon lemon extract

Directions:

1. In a bowl, add the coconut milk and beat until smooth.
2. Add the remaining ingredients and beat until sugar is dissolved.
3. Transfer the mixture into an empty Ninja CREAMi pint container.
4. Cover the container with storage lid and freeze for 24 hours.
5. After 24 hours, remove the lid from container and arrange into the Outer Bowl of Ninja CREAMi.
6. Install the Creamerizer Paddle onto the lid of Outer Bowl.
7. Then rotate the lid clockwise to lock.
8. Press Power button to turn on the unit.
9. Then press Ice Cream button.
10. When the program is completed, turn the Outer Bowl and release it from the machine.
11. Transfer the ice cream into serving bowls and serve immediately.

Nutrition Info:

- InfoCalories: 280,Fat: 18.3g,Carbohydrates: 28.2g,Protein: 1.5.

Carrot Ice Cream

Servings: 2
Cooking Time: 1 Minutes
Ingredients:
- 1 C. heavy cream
- ½ C. carrot juice
- 1/3 C. light brown sugar
- 2 tbsp. cream cheese frosting
- 1 tsp. vanilla extract
- 1 tsp. ground cinnamon

Directions:
1. In a bowl, add all ingredients and beat until well combined.
2. Transfer the mixture into an empty Ninja CREAMi pint container.
3. Cover the container with the storage lid and freeze for 24 hours
4. After 24 hours, remove the lid from container and arrange into the outer bowl of Ninja CREAMi.
5. Install the "Creamerizer Paddle" onto the lid of outer bowl.
6. Then rotate the lid clockwise to lock.
7. Press "Power" button to turn on the unit.
8. Then press "ICE CREAM" button.
9. When the program is completed, turn the outer bowl and release it from the machine.
10. Transfer the ice cream into serving bowls and serve immediately.

Nutrition Info:
- InfoCalories: 185,Carbohydrates: 18.4g,Protein: 0.8g,Fat: 12.4g,Sodium: 36m.

Fruit Carrot Ice Cream

Servings: 4
Cooking Time:x
Ingredients:
- ¾ cup heavy cream
- ½ cup milk
- ⅓ cup orange juice
- ¾ cup sugar
- ¼ cup frozen carrots
- ¼ cup pineapple chunks

Directions:
1. In a bowl, add the heavy cream, milk, orange juice and sugar and beat until sugar is dissolved.
2. In an empty Ninja CREAMi pint container, place the carrots and pineapple chunks and top with milk mixture.
3. Cover the container with storage lid and freeze for 24 hours.
4. After 24 hours, remove the lid from container and arrange into the Outer Bowl of Ninja CREAMi.
5. Install the Creamerizer Paddle onto the lid of Outer Bowl.
6. Then rotate the lid clockwise to lock.
7. Press Power button to turn on the unit.
8. Then press Ice Cream button.
9. When the program is completed, turn the Outer Bowl and release it from the machine.
10. Transfer the ice cream into serving bowls and serve immediately.

Nutrition Info:
- InfoCalories: 250,Fat: 9g,Carbohydrates: 43.5g,Protein: 1.7.

Super Lemon Ice Cream

Servings: 5
Cooking Time: 24 Hours And 20 Minutes
Ingredients:
- 1 cup heavy whipping cream
- ½ cup half-and-half cream
- ½ cup white sugar
- 1 tablespoon grated lemon zest
- 2 egg yolks
- ¼ cup fresh lemon juice

Directions:
1. On low heat, whisk together the heavy cream, half-and-half cream, sugar, and lemon zest in a saucepan until the sugar is dissolved.
2. In a mixing dish, whisk together the egg yolks.
3. Stir in a few tablespoons of the cream mixture at a time into the eggs. This will assist in bringing the eggs up to temperature without them becoming scrambled. Return the egg mixture to the bowl with the cream mixture.
4. Pour the mixture into an empty ninja CREAMi Pint container, add lemon, and freeze for 24 hours.
5. After 24 hours, remove the Pint from the freezer. Remove the lid.
6. Place the Ninja CREAMi Pint into the outer bowl. Place the outer bowl with the Pint in it into the ninja CREAMi machine and turn until the outer bowl locks into place. Push the ICE CREAM button.
7. Once the ICE CREAM function has ended, turn the outer bowl and release it from the ninja CREAMi machine.

Nutrition Info:
- InfoCalories 316,Protein 3.7g,Carbohydrate 27g,Fat 22g,Sodium 36mg.

Carrot Cheesecake Ice Cream

Servings: 4
Cooking Time:x
Ingredients:
- 1 cup heavy cream
- ½ cup carrot juice
- ⅓ cup light brown sugar
- 2 tablespoons cream cheese frosting
- 1 teaspoon vanilla extract
- 1 teaspoon ground cinnamon

Directions:
1. In a bowl, add all ingredients and beat until well combined.
2. Transfer the mixture into an empty Ninja CREAMi pint container.
3. Cover the container with storage lid and freeze for 24 hours.
4. After 24 hours, remove the lid from container and arrange into the Outer Bowl of Ninja CREAMi.
5. Install the Creamerizer Paddle onto the lid of Outer Bowl.
6. Then rotate the lid clockwise to lock.
7. Press Power button to turn on the unit.
8. Then press Ice Cream button.
9. When the program is completed, turn the Outer Bowl and release it from the machine.
10. Transfer the ice cream into serving bowls and serve immediately.

Nutrition Info:
- InfoCalories: 185,Fat: 12.4g,Carbohydrates: 18.4g,Protein: 0.8.

Cinnamon Red Hot Ice Cream

Servings: 5
Cooking Time: 24 Hours And 10 Minutes
Ingredients:

- 2 cups heavy whipping cream, divided
- 1 egg yolk
- 1 cup half-and-half
- ½ cup Red Hot candies

Directions:

1. In a mixing bowl, whisk together 1 cup of cream and the egg yolks until smooth.
2. In another large bowl, combine the half-and-half, 1 cup cream, and Red Hot candies. Whisk with a wooden spoon until the candies dissolve, about 5 to 10 minutes.
3. Pour the cream-egg mixture into the candy mixture and stir to incorporate.
4. Pour the mixture into an empty ninja CREAMi Pint container and freeze for 24 hours.
5. After 24 hours, remove the Pint from the freezer. Remove the lid.
6. Place the Ninja CREAMi Pint into the outer bowl. Place the outer bowl with the Pint in it into the ninja CREAMi machine and turn until the outer bowl locks into place. Push the ICE CREAM button.
7. Once the ICE CREAM function has ended, turn the outer bowl and release it from the ninja CREAMi machine.

Nutrition Info:

- InfoCalories 322,Protein 3g,Carbohydrate 24.5g,Fat 24g,Sodium 106mg.

French Vanilla Ice Cream

Servings:4
Cooking Time:x
Ingredients:

- 4 large egg yolks
- 1 tablespoon light corn syrup
- ¼ cup plus 1 tablespoon granulated sugar
- ⅓ cup whole milk
- 1 cup heavy (whipping) cream
- 1 teaspoon vanilla extract

Directions:

1. Fill a large bowl with ice water and set it aside.
2. In a small saucepan, whisk together the egg yolks, corn syrup, and sugar until the mixture is fully combined and the sugar is dissolved. Do not do this over heat.
3. Whisk in the milk, heavy cream, and vanilla until combined.
4. Place the pan over medium heat. Cook, stirring constantly with a rubber spatula, until the temperature reaches 165°F to 175°F on an instant-read thermometer.
5. Remove the pan from the heat and pour the base through a fine-mesh strainer into a clean CREAMi Pint. Carefully place the container in the prepared ice water bath, making sure the water doesn't spill into the base.
6. Once the base has cooled, place the storage lid on the pint and freeze for 24 hours.
7. Remove the CREAMi Pint from the freezer and take off the lid. Place the pint in the outer bowl of your Ninja CREAMi, install the Creamerizer Paddle in the outer bowl lid, and lock the lid assembly onto the outer bowl. Place the bowl assembly on the motor base, and twist the handle to the right to raise the platform and lock it in place. Select the Ice Cream function.
8. Once the machine has finished processing, remove the ice cream from the pint. Serve immediately.

Blueberry Ice Cream

Servings: 4
Cooking Time:x
Ingredients:
- 1 cup blueberries
- ½ cup vanilla whole milk Greek yogurt
- ¼ cup milk
- 2 tablespoons honey
- 2 tablespoons chia seeds

Directions:
1. In a bowl, add all ingredients and eat until well combined.
2. Transfer the mixture into an empty Ninja CREAMi pint container.
3. Cover the container with storage lid and freeze for 24 hours.
4. After 24 hours, remove the lid from container and arrange into the Outer Bowl of Ninja CREAMi.
5. Install the Creamerizer Paddle onto the lid of Outer Bowl.
6. Then rotate the lid clockwise to lock.
7. Press Power button to turn on the unit.
8. Then press Ice Cream button.
9. When the program is completed, turn the Outer Bowl and release it from the machine.
10. Transfer the ice cream into serving bowls and serve immediately.

Nutrition Info:
- InfoCalories: 115,Fat: 4g,Carbohydrates: 19.4g,Protein: 3.1.

Fruity Carrot Ice Cream

Servings: 4
Cooking Time:x
Ingredients:
- ¾ C. heavy cream
- ½ C. milk
- 1/3 C. orange juice
- ¾ C. sugar
- ¼ C. frozen carrots
- ¼ C. pineapple chunks

Directions:
1. In a bowl, add the heavy cream, milk, orange juice and sugar and beat until well combined.
2. In an empty Ninja CREAMi pint container, place the carrots and pineapple chunks and top with milk mixture.
3. Cover the container with the storage lid and freeze for 24 hours.
4. After 24 hours, remove the lid from container and arrange into the outer bowl of Ninja CREAMi.
5. Install the "Creamerizer Paddle" onto the lid of outer bowl.
6. Then rotate the lid clockwise to lock.
7. Press "Power" button to turn on the unit.
8. Then press "ICE CREAM" button.
9. When the program is completed, turn the outer bowl and release it from the machine.
10. Transfer the ice cream into serving bowls and serve immediately.

Nutrition Info:
- InfoCalories: 250,Carbohydrates: 43.5g,Protein: 1.7g,Fat: 9g,Sodium: 26m.

Sorbet Recipes

Strawberry Sorbet

Servings: 4
Cooking Time:x
Ingredients:
- 6 ounces daiquiri mix
- 2 ounces rum
- ½ cup frozen strawberries
- ½ cup simple syrup

Directions:
1. In an empty Ninja CREAMi pint container, add all the ingredients and mix well.
2. Cover the container with storage lid and freeze for 24 hours.
3. After 24 hours, remove the lid from container and arrange into the Outer Bowl of Ninja CREAMi.
4. Install the Creamerizer Paddle onto the lid of Outer Bowl.
5. Then rotate the lid clockwise to lock.
6. Press Power button to turn on the unit.
7. Then press Sorbet button.
8. When the program is completed, turn the Outer Bowl and release it from the machine.
9. Transfer the sorbet into serving bowls and serve immediately.

Nutrition Info:
- InfoCalories: 330,Fat: 0.1g,Carbohydrates: 72.6g,Protein: 0.1.

Acai & Fruit Sorbet

Servings: 4
Cooking Time:x
Ingredients:
- 1 packet frozen acai
- ½ cup blackberries
- ½ cup banana, peeled and sliced
- ¼ cup granulated sugar
- 1 cup water

Directions:
1. In a high-speed blender, add all the ingredients and pulse until smooth.
2. Transfer the mixture into an empty Ninja CREAMi pint container.
3. Cover the container with storage lid and freeze for 24 hours.
4. After 24 hours, remove the lid from container and arrange into the Outer Bowl of Ninja CREAMi.
5. Install the Creamerizer Paddle onto the lid of Outer Bowl.
6. Then rotate the lid clockwise to lock.
7. Press Power button to turn on the unit.
8. Then press Sorbet button.
9. When the program is completed, turn the Outer Bowl and release it from the machine.
10. Transfer the sorbet into serving bowls and serve immediately.

Nutrition Info:
- InfoCalories: 86,Fat: 0.2g,Carbohydrates: 22.3g,Protein: 0.5.

Grapes Sorbet

Servings: 4
Cooking Time:x
Ingredients:
- ¾ C. frozen grape juice concentrate
- 1½ C. water
- 1 tbsp. fresh lemon juice

Directions:
1. In a bowl, add all the ingredients and with a wire whisk, beat until well combined.
2. Transfer the mixture into an empty Ninja CREAMi pint container.
3. Cover the container with the storage lid and freeze for 24 hours.
4. After 24 hours, remove the lid from container and arrange into the outer bowl of Ninja CREAMi.
5. Install the "Creamerizer Paddle" onto the lid of outer bowl.
6. Then rotate the lid clockwise to lock.
7. Press "Power" button to turn on the unit.
8. Then press "SORBET" button.
9. When the program is completed, turn the outer bowl and release it from the machine.
10. Transfer the sorbet into serving bowls and serve immediately.

Nutrition Info:
- InfoCalories: 25,Carbohydrates: 6.1g,Protein: 0.1g,Fat: 0.1g,Sodium: 4m.

Lime Beer Sorbet

Servings: 4
Cooking Time:x
Ingredients:
- ¾ C. beer
- 2/3 C. water
- ½ C. fresh lime juice
- ¼ C. granulated sugar

Directions:
1. In a high-speed blender, add all the ingredients and pulse until smooth.
2. Set aside for about 5 minutes.
3. Transfer the mixture into an empty Ninja CREAMi pint container.
4. Cover the container with the storage lid and freeze for 24 hours.
5. After 24 hours, remove the lid from container and arrange into the outer bowl of Ninja CREAMi.
6. Install the "Creamerizer Paddle" onto the lid of outer bowl.
7. Then rotate the lid clockwise to lock.
8. Press "Power" button to turn on the unit.
9. Then press "SORBET" button.
10. When the program is completed, turn the outer bowl and release it from the machine
11. Transfer the sorbet into serving bowls and serve immediately.

Nutrition Info:
- InfoCalories: 69,Carbohydrates: 14.4g,Protein: 0.2g,Fat: 0g,Sodium: 3m.

Pomegranate & Blueberry Sorbet

Servings: 4
Cooking Time:x
Ingredients:

- 1 can blueberries in light syrup
- ½ cup pomegranate juice

Directions:

1. In an empty Ninja CREAMi pint container, place the blueberries and top with syrup
2. Add in the pomegranate juice and stir to combine.
3. Cover the container with storage lid and freeze for 24 hours.
4. After 24 hours, remove the lid from container and arrange into the Outer bowl of Ninja CREAMi.
5. Install the Creamerizer Paddle onto the lid of Outer Bowl.
6. Then rotate the lid clockwise to lock.
7. Press Power button to turn on the unit.
8. Then press Sorbet button.
9. When the program is completed, turn the Outer Bowl and release it from the machine.
10. Transfer the sorbet into serving bowls and serve immediately.

Nutrition Info:

- InfoCalories: 101,Fat: 0.4g,Carbohydrates: 25.2g,Protein: 0.8.

Strawberry & Beet Sorbet

Servings: 4
Cooking Time:x
Ingredients:

- 2 2/3 C. strawberries, hulled and quartered
- 1/3 C. cooked beets, quartered
- 1/3 C. granulated sugar
- 1/3 C. orange juice

Directions:

1. In a high-speed blender, add mangoes and beets and pulse until smooth.
2. Through a fine-mesh strainer, strain the mango puree into a large bowl.
3. Add the sugar and orange juice and and stir to combine.
4. Transfer the mixture into an empty Ninja CREAMi pint container.
5. Cover the container with the storage lid and freeze for 24 hours.
6. After 24 hours, remove the lid from container and arrange into the outer bowl of Ninja CREAMi.
7. Install the "Creamerizer Paddle" onto the lid of outer bowl.
8. Then rotate the lid clockwise to lock.
9. Press "Power" button to turn on the unit.
10. Then press "SORBET" button.
11. When the program is completed, turn the outer bowl and release it from the machine.
12. Transfer the sorbet into serving bowls and serve immediately.

Nutrition Info:

- InfoCalories: 109,Carbohydrates: 27,6g,Protein: 1g,Fat: 0.4g,Sodium: 12m.

Banana Sorbet

Servings: 2
Cooking Time: 24 Hours And 5 Minutes
Ingredients:
- 1 frozen banana
- 1 teaspoon cold water
- 2 teaspoons caramel sauce

Directions:
1. Add the banana, water, and caramel sauce into the ninja CREAMi Pint container and freeze on a level surface in a cold freezer for a full 24 hours.
2. After 24 hours, remove the Pint from the freezer. Remove the lid.
3. Place the Ninja CREAMi Pint into the outer bowl. Place the outer bowl with the Pint in it into the ninja CREAMi machine and turn until the outer bowl locks into place. Push the SORBET button. During the SORBET function, the sorbet will mix together and become very creamy. This should take approximately 2 minutes.
4. Once the SORBET function has ended, turn the outer bowl and release it from the ninja CREAMi machine.

Nutrition Info:
- InfoCalories 70,Protein 0.7g,Carbohydrate 18g,Fat 0.2g,Sodium 25mg.

Lemony Herb Sorbet

Servings: 4
Cooking Time: 6 Minutes
Ingredients:
- ½ cup water
- ¼ cup granulated sugar
- 2 large fresh dill sprigs, stemmed
- 2 large fresh basil sprigs, stemmed
- 1 cup ice water
- 2 tablespoons fresh lemon juice

Directions:
1. In a small saucepan, add sugar and water and over medium heat and cook for about five minutes or until the sugar is dissolved, stirring continuously.
2. Stir in the herb sprigs and remove from the heat.
3. Add the ice water and lemon juice and stir to combine.
4. Transfer the mixture into an empty Ninja CREAMi pint container.
5. Cover the container with storage lid and freeze for 24 hours.
6. After 24 hours, remove the lid from container and arrange into the Outer Bowl of Ninja CREAMi.
7. Install the Creamerizer Paddle onto the lid of Outer Bowl.
8. Then rotate the lid clockwise to lock.
9. Press Power button to turn on the unit.
10. Then press Sorbet button.
11. When the program is completed, turn the Outer Bowl and release it from the machine.
12. Transfer the sorbet into serving bowls and serve immediately.

Nutrition Info:
- InfoCalories: 51,Fat: 0.1g,Carbohydrates: 13.1g,Protein: 0.2.

Cherry-berry Rosé Sorbet

Servings: 3
Cooking Time: 24 Hours And 10 Minutes
Ingredients:

- 2 cups frozen cherry-berry fruit blend
- ½ cup rosé wine, or as needed
- ¼ cup white sugar, or to taste
- ¼ medium lemon, juiced

Directions:
1. Add all ingredients to a bowl and mix until the sugar dissolves. Place the mixture in the ninja CREAMi Pint container and freeze on a level surface in a cold freezer for a full 24 hours.
2. After 24 hours, remove the Pint from the freezer. Remove the lid.
3. Place the Ninja CREAMi Pint into the outer bowl. Place the outer bowl with the Pint in it into the ninja CREAMi machine and turn until the outer bowl locks into place. Push the SORBET button. During the SORBET function, the sorbet will mix together and become very creamy. This should take approximately 2 minutes.
4. Once the SORBET function has ended, turn the outer bowl and release it from the ninja CREAMi machine.
5. Your sorbet is ready to eat! Enjoy!

Nutrition Info:

- InfoCalories 186,Protein 1.5g,Carbohydrate 40g,Fat 0.2g,Sodium 4.9mg.

Strawberries & Champagne Sorbet

Servings: 3
Cooking Time: 24 Hours And 15 Minutes
Ingredients:

- 1 packet strawberry-flavored gelatin (such as Jell-O)
- ¾ cup boiling water
- ½ cup light corn syrup
- 3 fluid ounces champagne
- 1 egg whites, slightly beaten

Directions:
1. Dissolve the gelatin in boiling water in a bowl. Beat in the corn syrup, champagne, and egg whites.
2. Put the mixture into the ninja CREAMi Pint container and freeze on a level surface in a cold freezer for a full 24 hours.
3. After 24 hours, remove the Pint from the freezer. Remove the lid.
4. Place the Ninja CREAMi Pint into the outer bowl. Place the outer bowl with the Pint in it into the ninja CREAMi machine and turn until the outer bowl locks into place. Push the SORBET button. During the SORBET function, the sorbet will mix together and become very creamy. This should take approximately 2 minutes.
5. Once the SORBET function has ended, turn the outer bowl and release it from the ninja CREAMi machine.
6. Your sorbet is ready to eat! Enjoy!

Nutrition Info:

- InfoCalories 196,Protein 2.5g,Carbohydrate 46g,Fat 5g,Sodium 106mg.

Blueberry & Pomegranate Sorbet

Servings: 4
Cooking Time:x
Ingredients:

- 1 can blueberries in light syrup
- ½ C. pomegranate juice

Directions:
1. In an empty Ninja CREAMi pint container, place the blueberries and top with syrup.
2. Add in the pomegranate juice and stir to combine.
3. Cover the container with the storage lid and freeze for 24 hours.
4. After 24 hours, remove the lid from container and arrange into the outer bowl of Ninja CREAMi.
5. Install the "Creamerizer Paddle" onto the lid of outer bowl.
6. Then rotate the lid clockwise to lock
7. Press "Power" button to turn on the unit.
8. Then press "SORBET" button.
9. When the program is completed, turn the outer bowl and release it from the machine.
10. Transfer the sorbet into serving bowls and serve immediately.

Nutrition Info:

- InfoCalories: 101,Carbohydrates: 25.2g,Protein: 0.8g,Fat: 0.4g,Sodium: 4m.

Lime Sorbet

Servings: 4
Cooking Time:x
Ingredients:

- ¾ cup beer
- ⅔ cup water
- ½ cup fresh lime juice
- ¼ cup granulated sugar

Directions:

1. In a high-speed blender, add all the ingredients and pulse until smooth.
2. Set aside for about five minutes.
3. Transfer the mixture into an empty Ninja CREAMi pint container.
4. Cover the container with storage lid and freeze for 24 hours.
5. After 24 hours, remove the lid from container and arrange into the Outer Bowl of Ninja CREAMi.
6. Install the Creamerizer Paddle onto the lid of Outer Bowl.
7. Then rotate the lid clockwise to lock.
8. Press Power button to turn on the unit.
9. Then press Sorbet button.
10. When the program is completed, turn the Outer Bowl and release it from the machine.
11. Transfer the sorbet into serving bowls and serve immediately.

Nutrition Info:

- InfoCalories: 69,Fat: 0g,Carbohydrates: 14.4g,Protein: 0.2.

Grape Sorbet

Servings: 4
Cooking Time:x
Ingredients:

- ¾ cup frozen grape juice concentrate
- 1½ cups water
- 1 tablespoon fresh lemon juice

Directions:

1. In a bowl, add all the ingredients and beat until well combined.
2. Transfer the mixture into an empty Ninja CREAMi pint container.
3. Cover the container with storage lid and freeze for 24 hours.
4. After 24 hours, remove the lid from container and arrange into the Outer Bowl of Ninja CREAMi.
5. Install the Creamerizer Paddle onto the lid of Outer Bowl.
6. Then rotate the lid clockwise to lock.
7. Press Power button to turn on the unit.
8. Then press Sorbet button.
9. When the program is completed, turn the Outer Bowl and release it from the machine.
10. Transfer the sorbet into serving bowls and serve immediately.

Nutrition Info:

- InfoCalories: 25,Fat: 0.1g,Carbohydrates: 6.1g,Protein: 0.1.

Orange Sorbet

Servings: 4
Cooking Time:x
Ingredients:

- 1 can mandarin oranges with liquid

Directions:

1. Place the orange pieces into an empty Ninja CREAMi to the MAX FILL line.
2. Cover the orange pieces with liquid from the can.
3. Cover the container with the storage lid and freeze for 24 hours.
4. After 24 hours, remove the lid from container and arrange into the outer bowl of Ninja CREAMi.
5. Install the "Creamerizer Paddle" onto the lid of outer bowl.
6. Then rotate the lid clockwise to lock.
7. Press "Power" button to turn on the unit.
8. Then press "SORBET" button.
9. When the program is completed, turn the outer bowl and release it from the machine.
10. Transfer the sorbet into serving bowls and serve immediately.

Nutrition Info:

- InfoCalories: 52,Carbohydrates: 13.6g,Protein: 0.9g,Fat: 0g,Sodium: 7m.

Cherry Sorbet

Servings: 4
Cooking Time:x
Ingredients:

- 1½ C. cola
- 1/3 C. maraschino cherries
- 1/3 C. spiced rum
- ¼ C. water
- 1 tbsp. fresh lime juice

Directions:

1. In a high-speed blender, add all the ingredients and pulse until smooth.
2. Transfer the mixture into an empty Ninja CREAMi pint container.
3. Cover the container with the storage lid and freeze for 24 hours.
4. After 24 hours, remove the lid from container and arrange into the outer bowl of Ninja CREAMi.
5. Install the "Creamerizer Paddle" onto the lid of outer bowl.
6. Then rotate the lid clockwise to lock.
7. Press "Power" button to turn on the unit.
8. Then press "SORBET" button.
9. When the program is completed, turn the outer bowl and release it from the machine.
10. Transfer the sorbet into serving bowls and serve immediately.

Nutrition Info:

- InfoCalories: 95,Carbohydrates: 13.4g,Protein: 0.2g,Fat: 0.1g,Sodium: 4m.

Coconut Lime Sorbet

Servings: 5
Cooking Time: 24 Hours And 30 Minutes
Ingredients:

- 1 can coconut cream
- ½ cup coconut water
- ¼ cup lime juice
- ½ tablespoon lime zest
- ¼ teaspoon coconut extract (optional)

Directions:

1. Combine the coconut cream, coconut water, lime juice, lime zest, and coconut extract in a mixing bowl. Cover with plastic wrap and refrigerate for at least 1 hour, or until the flavors have melded.
2. Add the mixture to the Ninja CREAMi Pint container and freeze on a level surface in a cold freezer for a full 24 hours.
3. After 24 hours, remove the Pint from the freezer. Remove the lid.
4. Place the Ninja CREAMi Pint into the outer bowl. Place the outer bowl with the Pint in it into the ninja CREAMi machine and turn until the outer bowl locks into place. Push the SORBET button. During the SORBET function, the sorbet will mix together and become very creamy. This should take approximately 2 minutes.
5. Once the SORBET function has ended, turn the outer bowl and release it from the ninja CREAMi machine.
6. Your sorbet is ready to eat! Enjoy!

Nutrition Info:

- InfoCalories 194,Protein 1g,Carbohydrate 30g,Fat 9g,Sodium 36mg.

Raspberry Lime Sorbet

Servings: 4
Cooking Time:x
Ingredients:

- 2 C. fresh raspberries
- 5 oz. simple syrup
- 6 tbsp. fresh lime juice

Directions:

1. In an empty Ninja CREAMi pint container, add all the ingredients and mix well.
2. Cover the container with the storage lid and freeze for 24 hours.
3. After 24 hours, remove the lid from container and arrange into the outer bowl of Ninja CREAMi.
4. Install the "Creamerizer Paddle" onto the lid of outer bowl.
5. Then rotate the lid clockwise to lock.
6. Press "Power" button to turn on the unit.
7. Then press "SORBET" button.
8. When the program is completed, turn the outer bowl and release it from the machine.
9. Transfer the sorbet into serving bowls and serve immediately.

Nutrition Info:

- InfoCalories: 147,Carbohydrates: 37.3g,Protein: 0.7g,Fat: 0.4g,Sodium: 26m.

Strawberry & Kiwi Sorbet

Servings: 4
Cooking Time:x
Ingredients:

- 2 C. frozen sliced strawberries
- 4 kiwis, peeled and cut into 1-inch pieces
- ¼ C. agave nectar
- ¼ C. water

Directions:

1. In a high-speed blender, add all the ingredients and pulse until smooth.
2. Transfer the mixture into an empty Ninja CREAMi pint container.
3. Cover the container with the storage lid and freeze for 24 hours.
4. After 24 hours, remove the lid from container and arrange into the outer bowl of Ninja CREAMi.
5. Install the "Creamerizer Paddle" onto the lid of outer bowl.
6. Then rotate the lid clockwise to lock.
7. Press "Power" button to turn on the unit.
8. Then press "SORBET" button.
9. When the program is completed, turn the outer bowl and release it from the machine.
10. Transfer the sorbet into serving bowls and serve immediately.

Nutrition Info:

- InfoCalories: 131,Carbohydrates: 33.7g,Protein: 0.9g,Fat: 0.4g,Sodium: 3m.

Avocado Lime Sorbet

Servings: 4
Cooking Time: 5 Minutes
Ingredients:

- ¾ C. water
- 2 tbsp. light corn syrup
- Pinch of sea salt
- 2/3 C. granulated sugar
- 1 large ripe avocado, peeled, pitted and chopped
- 3 oz. fresh lime juice

Directions:

1. In a medium saucepan, add water, corn syrup and salt and beat until well combined.
2. Place the saucepan over medium heat.
3. Slowly add the sugar, continuously beating until well combined and bring to a boil.
4. Remove the saucepan from heat and set aside to cool completely.
5. In a high-speed blender, add the sugar mixture, avocado and lime juice and pulse until smooth.
6. Transfer the mixture into an empty Ninja CREAMi pint container.
7. Cover the container with the storage lid and freeze for 24 hours.
8. After 24 hours, remove the lid from container and arrange into the outer bowl of Ninja CREAMi.
9. Install the "Creamerizer Paddle" onto the lid of outer bowl.
10. Then rotate the lid clockwise to lock.
11. Press "Power" button to turn on the unit.
12. Then press "SORBET" button.
13. When the program is completed, turn the outer bowl and release it from the machine.
14. Transfer the sorbet into serving bowls and serve immediately.

Nutrition Info:

- InfoCalories: 244,Carbohydrates: 46g,Protein: 0.9g,Fat: 8.3g,Sodium: 64m.

Pineapple Rum Sorbet

Servings: 4
Cooking Time:x
Ingredients:

- ¾ C. piña colada mix
- ¼ C. rum
- 2 tbsp. granulated sugar
- 1½ C. frozen pineapple chunks

Directions:

1. In a high-speed blender, add all the ingredients and pulse until smooth.
2. Transfer the mixture into an empty Ninja CREAMi pint container.
3. Cover the container with the storage lid and freeze for 24 hours.
4. After 24 hours, remove the lid from container and arrange into the outer bowl of Ninja CREAMi.
5. Install the "Creamerizer Paddle" onto the lid of outer bowl.
6. Then rotate the lid clockwise to lock.
7. Press "Power" button to turn on the unit.
8. Then press "SORBET" button.
9. When the program is completed, turn the outer bowl and release it from the machine.
10. Transfer the sorbet into serving bowls and serve immediately.

Nutrition Info:

- InfoCalories: 102,Carbohydrates: 17.6g,Protein: 0.6g,Fat: 0.2g,Sodium: 1m.

Plum Sorbet

Servings: 4
Cooking Time:x
Ingredients:

- 1 can plums

Directions:

1. Place the plums into an empty Ninja CREAMi pint container.
2. Cover the container with storage lid and freeze for 24 hours.
3. After 24 hours, remove the lid from container and arrange into the Outer Bowl of Ninja CREAMi.
4. Install the Creamerizer Paddle onto the lid of Outer Bowl.
5. Then rotate the lid clockwise to lock.
6. Press Power button to turn on the unit.
7. Then press Sorbet button.
8. When the program is completed, turn the Outer Bowl and release it from the machine.
9. Transfer the sorbet into serving bowls and serve immediately.

Nutrition Info:

- InfoCalories: 150,Fat: 1g,Carbohydrates: 40g,Protein: 2.5.

Kiwi & Strawberry Sorbet

Servings: 4
Cooking Time:x
Ingredients:

- 2 cups frozen sliced strawberries
- 4 kiwis, peeled and cut into 1-inch pieces
- ¼ cup agave nectar
- ¼ cup water

Directions:

1. In a high-speed blender, add all the ingredients and pulse until smooth.
2. Transfer the mixture into an empty Ninja CREAMi pint container.
3. Cover the container with storage lid and freeze for 24 hours.
4. After 24 hours, remove the lid from container and arrange into the Outer Bowl of Ninja CREAMi.
5. Install the Creamerizer Paddle onto the lid of Outer Bowl.
6. Then rotate the lid clockwise to lock.
7. Press Power button to turn on the unit.
8. Then press Sorbet button.
9. When the program is completed, turn the Outer Bowl and release it from the machine.
10. Transfer the sorbet into serving bowls and serve immediately.

Nutrition Info:

- InfoCalories: 131,Fat: 0.4g,Carbohydrates: 33.7g,Protein: 0.9.

Mixed Berries Sorbet

Servings: 4
Cooking Time:x
Ingredients:

- 1 cup blueberries
- 1 cup raspberries
- 1 cup strawberries, hulled and quartered

Directions:

1. In an empty Ninja CREAMi pint container, place the berries and with a potato masher, mash until well combined.
2. Cover the container with storage lid and freeze for 24 hours.
3. After 24 hours, remove the lid from container and arrange into the outer bowl of Ninja CREAMi.
4. Install the Creamerizer Paddle onto the lid of Outer Bowl.
5. Then rotate the lid clockwise to lock.
6. Press Power button to turn on the unit.
7. Then press Sorbet button.
8. When the program is completed, turn the Outer Bowl and release it from the machine.
9. Transfer the sorbet into serving bowls and serve immediately.

Nutrition Info:

- InfoCalories: 48,Fat: .40g,Carbohydrates: 11.7g,Protein: 0.9.

Peach Sorbet

Servings: 4
Cooking Time:x
Ingredients:

- 1 cup passionfruit seltzer
- 3 tablespoons agave nectar
- 1 can peaches in heavy syrup, drained

Directions:

1. In a bowl, add the seltzer and agave and beat until agave is dissolved.
2. Place the peaches into an empty Ninja CREAMi pint container and top with seltzer mixture.
3. Cover the container with storage lid and freeze for 24 hours.
4. After 24 hours, remove the lid from container and arrange into the Outer Bowl of Ninja CREAMi.
5. Install the Creamerizer Paddle onto the lid of Outer Bowl.
6. Then rotate the lid clockwise to lock.
7. Press Power button to turn on the unit.
8. Then press Sorbet button.
9. When the program is completed, turn the Outer Bowl and release it from the machine.
10. Transfer the sorbet into serving bowls and serve immediately.

Nutrition Info:

- InfoCalories: 271,Fat: 1.5g,Carbohydrates: 65.4g,Protein: 5.3.

Chocolate Sorbet

Servings: 2
Cooking Time: 24 Hours And 5 Minutes
Ingredients:

- ½ cup white sugar
- ⅓ cup unsweetened cocoa powder
- 1 pinch sea salt
- 1 cups water
- 1 tablespoon brewed espresso or strong coffee
- ½ teaspoon almond extract
- 1 tablespoon coffee liqueur

Directions:

1. Mix the sugar, cocoa powder, and sea salt in a large saucepan. Stir in water, espresso, and almond extract. Once the sugar has dissolved and the mixture is smooth, stir in the coffee liqueur.
2. Pour into a ninja CREAMi Pint container and freeze on a level surface in a cold freezer for a full 24 hours.
3. After 24 hours, remove the Pint from the freezer. Remove the lid.
4. Place the Ninja CREAMi Pint into the outer bowl. Place the outer bowl with the Pint in it into the ninja CREAMi machine and turn until the outer bowl locks into place. Push the SORBET button. During the SORBET function, the sorbet will mix together and become very creamy. This should take approximately 2 minutes.
5. Once the SORBET function has ended, turn the outer bowl and release it from the ninja CREAMi machine.

Nutrition Info:

- InfoCalories 256,Protein 3g,Carbohydrate 61g,Fat 2g,Sodium 63mg.

Smoothie Bowls Recipes

Chocolate Pumpkin Smoothie Bowl

Servings:4
Cooking Time:x
Ingredients:

- ½ cup canned pumpkin puree
- 2 tablespoons unsweetened cocoa powder
- 1 teaspoon pumpkin spice seasoning
- 2 ripe bananas, cut in ½-inch pieces
- 1 tablespoon agave nectar
- ¼ cup whole milk

Directions:

1. In a small bowl, stir together the pumpkin puree, cocoa powder, and pumpkin spice until well combined. Pour the base into a clean CREAMi Pint. Mix in the bananas, agave, and milk until everything is fully combined and the bananas are coated. Place the storage lid on the container and freeze for 24 hours.
2. Remove the pint from the freezer and take off the lid. Place the pint in the outer bowl of your Ninja CREAMi, install the Creamerizer Paddle in the outer bowl lid, and lock the lid assembly onto the outer bowl. Place the bowl assembly on the motor base, and twist the handle to the right to raise the platform and lock it in place. Select the Smoothie Bowl function.
3. Once the machine has finished processing, remove the smoothie bowl from the pint. Serve immediately with your desired toppings.

Simple Smoothie Bowl

Servings:2
Cooking Time:x
Ingredients:

- 1 bottle fruit smoothie beverage

Directions:

1. Pour the smoothie beverage into a clean CREAMi Pint. Place the storage lid on the container and freeze for 24 hours
2. Remove the pint from the freezer and take off the lid. Place the pint in the outer bowl of your Ninja CREAMi, install the Creamerizer Paddle in the outer bowl lid, and lock the lid assembly onto the outer bowl. Place the bowl assembly on the motor base, and twist the handle to the right to raise the platform and lock it in place. Select the Smoothie Bowl function.
3. Once the machine has finished processing, remove the smoothie bowl from the pint. Serve immediately with desired toppings.

Mango & Raspberry Smoothie Bowl

Servings: 2
Cooking Time:x
Ingredients:

- ¾ cup frozen mango chunks
- ½ cup frozen raspberries
- ½ cup whole milk Greek yogurt
- 2 tablespoons avocado flesh
- 1 tablespoon agave nectar

Directions:

1. In a large bowl, add all the ingredients and mix well.
2. Transfer the mixture into an empty Ninja CREAMi pint container.
3. Cover the container with storage lid and freeze for 24 hours.
4. After 24 hours, remove the lid from container and arrange into the Outer Bowl of Ninja CREAMi.
5. Install the Creamerizer Paddle onto the lid of Outer Bowl.
6. Then rotate the lid clockwise to lock.
7. Press Power button to turn on the unit.
8. Then press Smoothie Bowl button.
9. When the program is completed, turn the Outer Bowl and release it from the machine.
10. Transfer the smoothie into serving bowls and serve immediately.

Nutrition Info:

- InfoCalories: 163,Fat: 5g,Carbohydrates: 27.4g,Protein: 3.9.

Orange & Mango Smoothie Bowl

Servings: 2
Cooking Time:x
Ingredients:

- 1 C. frozen mango chunks
- 1 C. plain whole milk yogurt
- ¼ C. fresh orange juice
- 2 tbsp. maple syrup
- ½ tsp. ground turmeric
- 1/8 tsp. ground cinnamon
- 1/8 tsp. ground ginger
- Pinch of ground black pepper

Directions:

1. In a high-speed blender, add all ingredients and pulse until smooth
2. Transfer the mixture into an empty Ninja CREAMi pint container.
3. Cover the container with the storage lid and freeze for 24 hours.
4. After 24 hours, remove the lid from container and arrange into the outer bowl of Ninja CREAMi.
5. Install the "Creamerizer Paddle" onto the lid of outer bowl.
6. Then rotate the lid clockwise to lock.
7. Press "Power" button to turn on the unit.
8. Then press "SMOOTHIE BOWL" button.
9. When the program is completed, turn the outer bowl and release it from the machine.
10. Transfer the smoothie into serving bowls and serve immediately.

Nutrition Info:

- InfoCalories: 188,Carbohydrates: 34.8g,Protein: 4.9g,Fat: 4.2g,Sodium: 94m.

Piña Colada Smoothie Bowl

Servings:4
Cooking Time:x
Ingredients:

- 1½ cups canned pineapple chunks in their juice
- ½ cup canned coconut milk
- 1 tablespoon agave nectar

Directions:

1. Pour the pineapple chunks in their juice, coconut milk, and agave into a clean CREAMi Pint and stir to combine. Place the storage lid on the container and freeze for 24 hours.
2. Remove the pint from the freezer and take off the lid. Place the pint in the outer bowl of your Ninja CREAMi, install the Creamerizer Paddle in the outer bowl lid, and lock the lid assembly onto the outer bowl. Place the bowl assembly on the motor base, and twist the handle to the right to raise the platform and lock it in place. Select the Smoothie Bowl function.
3. Once the machine has finished processing, remove the smoothie bowl from the pint. Serve immediately with your desired toppings.

Berries & Cherry Smoothie Bowl

Servings: 4
Cooking Time:x
Ingredients:

- 1 cup cranberry juice cocktail
- ¼ cup agave nectar
- 2 cups frozen cherry berry blend

Directions:

1. In a large bowl, add the agave nectar and cranberry juice cocktail and beat until well combined.
2. Place the cherry berry blend into an empty Ninja CREAMi pint container.
3. Top with cocktail mixture and stir to combine.
4. Cover the container with storage lid and freeze for 24 hours.
5. After 24 hours, remove the lid from container and arrange into the Outer Bowl of Ninja CREAMi.
6. Install the Creamerizer Paddle onto the lid of outer bowl.
7. Then rotate the lid clockwise to lock.
8. Press Power button to turn on the unit.
9. Then press Smoothie Bowl button.
10. When the program is completed, turn the Outer Bowl and release it from the machine.
11. Transfer the smoothie into serving bowls and serve immediately.

Nutrition Info:

- InfoCalories: 127,Fat: 0.3g,Carbohydrates: 1.5g,Protein: 0.5g fresh berries, oat.

Buttery Coffee Smoothie

Servings: 1
Cooking Time: 5 Minutes
Ingredients:

- 1 cup brewed coffee
- 2 large pasteurized egg yolks
- ¼ cup avocado
- ¼ cup ice cubes
- 1 tablespoon coconut sugar
- 2 tablespoons coconut oil, melted

Directions:

1. Combine the coffee, egg yolks, avocado, ice cubes, and coconut sugar in an empty ninja CREAMi Pint.
2. Place the Ninja CREAMi Pint into the outer bowl. Place the outer bowl with the Pint in it into the ninja CREAMi machine and turn until the outer bowl locks into place. Push the SMOOTHIE button. During the SMOOTHIE function, the ingredients will mix together and become very creamy.
3. Once the SMOOTHIE function has ended, turn the outer bowl and release it from the ninja CREAMi machine.
4. Scoop the smoothie into a tall glass.

Nutrition Info:

- InfoCalories 486,Protein 6.7g,Carbohydrate 19g,Fat 44g,Sodium 30mg.

Coffee Smoothie Bowl

Servings: 2
Cooking Time:x
Ingredients:

- 2 cups unsweetened vanilla almond milk
- ¼ cup instant coffee

Directions:

1. In a large bowl, add the almond milk and instant coffee mix and beat until well combine
2. Transfer the mixture into an empty Ninja CREAMi pint container.
3. Cover the container with storage lid and freeze for 24 hours.
4. After 24 hours, remove the lid from container and arrange into the Outer Bowl of Ninja CREAMi.
5. Install the Creamerizer Paddle onto the lid of Outer Bowl.
6. Then rotate the lid clockwise to lock.
7. Press Power button to turn on the unit.
8. Then press Smoothie Bowl button.
9. When the program is completed, turn the Outer Bowl and release it from the machine.
10. Transfer the smoothie into serving bowls and serve immediately.

Nutrition Info:

- InfoCalories: 40,Fat: 3.5g,Carbohydrates: 2g,Protein: 1.

Oat Banana Smoothie Bowl

Servings: 2
Cooking Time: 1 Minute
Ingredients:

- ½ cup water
- ¼ cup quick oats
- 1 cup vanilla Greek yogurt
- ½ cup banana, peeled and sliced
- 3 tablespoons honey

Directions:

1. In a small microwave-safe bowl, add the water and oats and microwave on High or about one minute.
2. Remove from the microwave and stir in the yogurt, banana and honey until well combined.
3. Transfer the mixture into an empty Ninja CREAMi pint container.
4. Cover the container with storage lid and freeze for 24 hours.
5. After 24 hours, remove the lid from container and arrange into the Outer Bowl of Ninja CREAMi.
6. Install the Creamerizer Paddle onto the lid of Outer Bowl.
7. Then rotate the lid clockwise to lock.
8. Press Power button to turn on the unit.
9. Then press Smoothie Bowl button.
10. When the program is completed, turn the Outer Bowl and release it from the machine.
11. Transfer the smoothie into serving bowls and serve with your favorite topping.

Nutrition Info:

- InfoCalories: 278,Fat: 2.7g,Carbohydrates: 55.7g,Protein: 10.9.

Three Fruit Smoothie Bowl

Servings: 2
Cooking Time:x
Ingredients:

- 1 C. frozen dragon fruit pieces
- ¾ C. fresh strawberries, hulled and quartered
- ¾ C. pineapple, cut in 1-inch pieces
- ½ C. low-fat plain yogurt
- 2 tbsp. agave nectar
- 1 tbsp. fresh lime juice

Directions:

1. In a large high-speed blender, add all the ingredients and pulse until smooth.
2. Transfer the mixture into an empty Ninja CREAMi pint container.
3. Cover the container with the storage lid and freeze for 24 hours.
4. After 24 hours, remove the lid from container and arrange into the outer bowl of Ninja CREAMi.
5. Install the "Creamerizer Paddle" onto the lid of outer bowl.
6. Then rotate the lid clockwise to lock.
7. Press "Power" button to turn on the unit.
8. Then press "SMOOTHIE BOWL" button.
9. When the program is completed, turn the outer bowl and release it from the machine.
10. Transfer the smoothie into serving bowls and serve immediately.

Nutrition Info:

- InfoCalories: 183,Carbohydrates: 40.5g,Protein: 4.5g,Fat: 1.2g,Sodium: 94m.

Avocado And Kale Smoothie Bowl

Servings:4
Cooking Time:x
Ingredients:

- 1 banana, cut into 1-inch pieces
- ½ ripe avocado, cut into 1-inch pieces
- 1 cup packed kale leaves
- 1 cup green apple pieces
- ¼ cup unsweetened coconut milk
- 2 tablespoons agave nectar

Directions:

1. Combine the banana, avocado, kale, apple, coconut milk, and agave in a blender. Blend on high for about 1 minute until smooth.
2. Pour the base into a clean CREAMi Pint. Place the storage lid on the container and freeze for 24 hours.
3. Remove the pint from the freezer and take off the lid. Place the pint in the outer bowl of your Ninja CREAMi, install the Creamerizer Paddle in the outer bowl lid, and lock the lid assembly onto the outer bowl. Place the bowl assembly on the motor base, and twist the handle to the right to raise the platform and lock it in place. Select the Smoothie Bowl function.
4. Once the machine has finished processing, remove the smoothie bowl from the pint. Serve immediately with your desired toppings.

Mango Smoothie Bowl

Servings: 4
Cooking Time:x
Ingredients:

- 2 cups ripe mango, peeled, pitted and cut into 1-inch pieces
- 1 can of unsweetened coconut milk

Directions:

1. Place the mango pieces into an empty Ninja CREAMi pint container.
2. Top with coconut milk and stir to combine.
3. Cover the container with storage lid and freeze for 24 hours.
4. After 24 hours, remove the lid from container and arrange into the Outer Bowl of Ninja CREAMi.
5. Install the Creamerizer Paddle onto the lid of Outer Bowl.
6. Then rotate the lid clockwise to lock.
7. Press Power button to turn on the unit.
8. Then press Smoothie Bowl button.
9. When the program is completed, turn the Outer Bowl and release it from the machine.
10. Transfer the smoothie into serving bowls and serve immediately.

Nutrition Info:

- InfoCalories: 198,Fat: 14g,Carbohydrates: 14.8g,Protein: 1..

Pineapple & Dragon Fruit Smoothie Bowl

Servings: 2
Cooking Time:x
Ingredients:

- 2 C. frozen dragon fruit chunks
- 2 cans pineapple juice

Directions:

1. Place the dragon fruit chunks and pineapple juice into an empty Ninja CREAMi pint container and stir to combine.
2. Cover the container with the storage lid and freeze for 24 hours.
3. After 24 hours, remove the lid from container and arrange into the outer bowl of Ninja CREAMi.
4. Install the "Creamerizer Paddle" onto the lid of outer bowl.
5. Then rotate the lid clockwise to lock.
6. Press "Power" button to turn on the unit.
7. Then press "SMOOTHIE BOWL" button.
8. When the program is completed, turn the outer bowl and release it from the machine.
9. Transfer the smoothie into serving bowls and serve immediately.

Nutrition Info:

- InfoCalories: 68,Carbohydrates: 17g,Protein: 0.3g,Fat: 0.1g,Sodium: 6m.

Papaya Smoothie Bowl

Servings: 2
Cooking Time:x
Ingredients:

- 2 C. ripe papaya, peeled and cut into 1-inch pieces
- 14 oz. whole milk
- 4-6 drops liquid stevia
- ¼ tsp. vanilla extract

Directions:

1. Place the mango pieces into an empty Ninja CREAMi pint container.
2. Top with coconut milk, stevia and vanilla extract and stir to combine.
3. Cover the container with the storage lid and freeze for 24 hours.
4. After 24 hours, remove the lid from container and arrange into the outer bowl of Ninja CREAMi.
5. Install the "Creamerizer Paddle" onto the lid of outer bowl.
6. Then rotate the lid clockwise to lock.
7. Press "Power" button to turn on the unit.
8. Then press "SMOOTHIE BOWL" button.
9. When the program is completed, turn the outer bowl and release it from the machine.
10. Transfer the smoothie into serving bowls and serve immediately.

Nutrition Info:

- InfoCalories: 183,Carbohydrates: 24.7g,Protein: 7.1g,Fat: 6.9g,Sodium: 91m.

Vodka Smoothie

Servings: 2
Cooking Time: 5 Minutes
Ingredients:

- 3 fluid ounces vodka
- 9 fluid ounces orange juice
- ½ cup frozen strawberries
- 2 scoops orange sherbet
- ½ cup crushed ice

Directions:

1. Mix the vodka, orange juice, strawberries, orange sherbet, and ice in an empty ninja CREAMi Pint.
2. Place the Ninja CREAMi Pint into the outer bowl. Place the outer bowl with the Pint in it into the ninja CREAMi machine and turn until the outer bowl locks into place. Push the SMOOTHIE button. During the SMOOTHIE function, the ingredients will mix together and become very creamy.
3. Once the SMOOTHIE function has ended, turn the outer bowl and release it from the ninja CREAMi machine.
4. Scoop the smoothie into glass cups.

Nutrition Info:

- InfoCalories 230,Protein 1.6g,Carbohydrate 30g,Fat 1.5g,Sodium 21.6mg.

Pumpkin Smoothie Bowl

Servings: 2
Cooking Time:x
Ingredients:

- 1 cup canned pumpkin puree
- ⅓ cup plain Greek yogurt
- 1½ tablespoons maple syrup
- 1 teaspoon vanilla extract
- 1 teaspoon pumpkin pie spice
- 1 frozen banana, peeled and cut in ½-inch pieces

Directions:

1. In an empty Ninja CREAMi pint container, add the pumpkin puree, yogurt, maple syrup, vanilla extract and pumpkin pie spice and mix well.
2. Add the banana pieces and stir to combine.
3. Transfer the mixture into an empty Ninja CREAMi pint container.
4. Arrange the container into the Outer Bowl of Ninja CREAMi.
5. Install the Creamerizer Paddle onto the lid of Outer Bowl.
6. Then rotate the lid clockwise to lock.
7. Press Power button to turn on the unit.
8. Then press Smoothie Bowl button.
9. When the program is completed, turn the Outer Bowl and release it from the machine.
10. Transfer the smoothie into serving bowls and serve immediately.

Nutrition Info:

- InfoCalories: 170,Fat: 0.7g,Carbohydrates: 35.8g,Protein: 7.5.

Strawberry Smoothie Bowl

Servings: 4
Cooking Time:x
Ingredients:

- 2 tablespoons vanilla protein powder
- ¼ cup agave nectar
- ¼ cup pineapple juice
- ½ cup whole milk
- 1 cup ripe banana, peeled and cut in ½-inch pieces
- 1 cup fresh strawberries, hulled and quartered

Directions:

1. In a large bowl, add the protein powder, agave nectar, pineapple juice and milk and beat until well combined.
2. Place the banana and strawberry into an empty Ninja CREAMi pint container and with the back of a spoon, firmly press the fruit below the Max Fill line.
3. Top with milk mixture and mix until well combined.
4. Cover the container with storage lid and freeze for 24 hours.
5. After 24 hours, remove the lid from container and arrange into the Outer Bowl of Ninja CREAMi.
6. Install the Creamerizer Paddle onto the lid of Outer Bowl.
7. Then rotate the lid clockwise to lock.
8. Press Power button to turn on the unit.
9. Then press Smoothie Bowl button.
10. When the program is completed, turn the Outer Bowl and release it from the machine.
11. Transfer the smoothie into serving bowls and serve immediately.

Nutrition Info:

- InfoCalories: 145,Fat: 1.3g,Carbohydrates: 31g,Protein: 4.7.

Pumpkin & Banana Smoothie Bowl

Servings: 2
Cooking Time:x
Ingredients:

- 1 C. canned pumpkin puree
- 1/3 C. plain Greek yogurt
- 1½ tbsp. maple syrup
- 1 tsp. vanilla extract
- 1 tsp. pumpkin pie spice
- 1 frozen banana, peeled and cut in ½-inch pieces

Directions:

1. In an empty Ninja CREAMi pint container, add the pumpkin puree, yogurt, maple syrup, vanilla extract, and pumpkin pie spice and mix well.
2. Add the banana pieces and stir to combine.
3. Transfer the mixture into an empty Ninja CREAMi pint container.
4. Arrange the container into the outer bowl of Ninja CREAMi.
5. Install the "Creamerizer Paddle" onto the lid of outer bowl.
6. Then rotate the lid clockwise to lock.
7. Press "Power" button to turn on the unit.
8. Then press "SMOOTHIE BOWL" button.
9. When the program is completed, turn the outer bowl and release it from the machine.
10. Transfer the smoothie into serving bowls and serve immediately.

Nutrition Info:

- InfoCalories: 170,Carbohydrates: 35.8g,Protein: 7.5g,Fat: 0.7g,Sodium: 28m.

Energy Elixir Smoothie

Servings: 1
Cooking Time: 5 Minutes
Ingredients:

- ½ cup spring salad greens
- ½ cup frozen red grapes
- ½ chopped frozen banana
- ½ cored and chopped frozen pear
- 2 tablespoons walnuts
- Water as needed

Directions:

1. Layer the salad greens, red grapes, banana, pear, walnuts, and enough water to cover the mixture in an empty ninja CREAMi Pint.
2. Place the Ninja CREAMi Pint into the outer bowl. Place the outer bowl with the Pint in it into the ninja CREAMi machine and turn until the outer bowl locks into place. Push the SMOOTHIE button. During the SMOOTHIE function, the ingredients will mix together and become very creamy.
3. Once the SMOOTHIE function has ended, turn the outer bowl and release it from the ninja CREAMi machine.
4. Scoop the smoothie into a glass.

Nutrition Info:

- InfoCalories 420,Protein 6g,Carbohydrate 84g,Fat 11g,Sodium 27.4mg.

Raspberry Smoothie Bowl

Servings: 4
Cooking Time:x
Ingredients:
- 1 cup brewed coffee
- ½ cup oat milk
- 2 tablespoons almond butter
- 1 cup fresh raspberries
- 1 large banana, peeled and sliced

Directions:
1. In a high-speed blender add all the ingredients and pulse until smooth.
2. Transfer the mixture into an empty Ninja CREAMi pint container.
3. Cover the container with storage lid and freeze for 24 hours.
4. After 24 hours, remove the lid from container and arrange into the Outer Bowl of Ninja CREAMi.
5. Install the Creamerizer Paddle onto the lid of Outer Bowl.
6. Then rotate the lid clockwise to lock.
7. Press Power button to turn on the unit.
8. Then press Smoothie Bowl button.
9. When the program is completed, turn the Outer Bowl and release it from the machine.
10. Transfer the smoothie into serving bowls and serve immediately.

Nutrition Info:
- InfoCalories: 108,Fat: 5.1g,Carbohydrates: 14.9g,Protein: 3.

Fruity Coffee Smoothie Bowl

Servings: 4
Cooking Time:x
Ingredients:
- 1 C. brewed coffee
- ½ C. oat milk
- 2 tbsp. almond butter
- 1 C. fresh raspberries
- 1 large banana, peeled and sliced

Directions:
1. In a high-speed blender add all the ingredients and pulse until smooth.
2. Transfer the mixture into an empty Ninja CREAMi pint container.
3. Cover the container with the storage lid and freeze for 24 hours.
4. After 24 hours, remove the lid from container and arrange into the outer bowl of Ninja CREAMi.
5. Install the "Creamerizer Paddle" onto the lid of outer bowl.
6. Then rotate the lid clockwise to lock.
7. Press "Power" button to turn on the unit.
8. Then press "SMOOTHIE BOWL" button.
9. When the program is completed, turn the outer bowl and release it from the machine.
10. Transfer the smoothie into serving bowls and serve immediately.

Nutrition Info:
- InfoCalories: 108,Carbohydrates: 14.9g,Protein: 3g,Fat: 5.1g,Sodium: 84m.

Gator Smoothies

Servings: 1
Cooking Time: 5 Minutes
Ingredients:
- 1 cup ice
- 1 cup grape-flavored sports drink
- 1 scoop vanilla ice cream

Directions:
1. Add the ice, sports drink, and ice cream into an empty ninja CREAMi Pint.
2. Place the Ninja CREAMi Pint into the outer bowl. Place the outer bowl with the Pint in it into the ninja CREAMi machine and turn until the outer bowl locks into place. Push the SMOOTHIE button. During the SMOOTHIE function, the ingredients will mix together and become very creamy.
3. Once the SMOOTHIE function has ended, turn the outer bowl and release it from the ninja CREAMi machine.
4. Pour into a tall glass.

Nutrition Info:
- InfoCalories 96,Protein 0.7g,Carbohydrate 18g,Fat 2.1g,Sodium 53.5mg.

Vanilla Cookie Smoothie

Servings: 2
Cooking Time: 5 Minutes
Ingredients:
- ¾ cup vanilla ice cream
- 2 lemon cream sandwich cookies
- ¼ cup milk

Directions:
1. Add the ice cream, smashed cookies, and milk to an empty ninja CREAMi Pint.
2. Place the Ninja CREAMi Pint into the outer bowl. Place the outer bowl with the Pint in it into the ninja CREAMi machine and turn until the outer bowl locks into place. Push the SMOOTHIE button. During the SMOOTHIE function, the ingredients will mix together and become very creamy.
3. Once the SMOOTHIE function has ended, turn the outer bowl and release it from the ninja CREAMi machine.
4. Pour the smoothies into tall glasses.

Nutrition Info:
- InfoCalories 237,Protein 3g,Carbohydrate 57g,Fat 2.4g,Sodium 18.3mg.

Green Fruity Smoothie Bowl

Servings: 2
Cooking Time:x

Ingredients:

- 1 banana, peeled and cut into 1-inch pieces
- ½ of avocado, peeled, pitted and cut into 1-inch pieces
- 1 C. fresh kale leaves
- 1 C. green apple, peeled, cored and cut into 1-inch pieces
- ¼ C. unsweetened coconut milk
- 2 tbsp. agave nectar

Directions:

1. In a large high-speed blender, add all the ingredients and pulse until smooth.
2. Transfer the mixture into an empty Ninja CREAMi pint container.
3. Cover the container with the storage lid and freeze for 24 hours.
4. After 24 hours, remove the lid from container and arrange into the outer bowl of Ninja CREAMi.
5. Install the "Creamerizer Paddle" onto the lid of outer bowl.
6. Then rotate the lid clockwise to lock.
7. Press "Power" button to turn on the unit.
8. Then press "SMOOTHIE BOWL" button.
9. When the program is completed, turn the outer bowl and release it from the machine.
10. Transfer the smoothie into serving bowls and serve immediately.

Nutrition Info:

- InfoCalories: 359,Carbohydrates: 54.4g,Protein: 3.6g,Fat: 17.3g,Sodium: 24m.

Strawberry-orange Creme Smoothie

Servings: 1
Cooking Time: 5 Minutes

Ingredients:

- 1 container Yoplait Greek 100 orange creme yogurt
- ½ cup fresh strawberries, hulled
- ¼ cup ice cubes (optional)
- ¼ cup orange juice

Directions:

1. Put all the ingredients into an empty ninja CREAMi Pint.
2. Place the Ninja CREAMi Pint into the outer bowl. Place the outer bowl with the Pint in it into the ninja CREAMi machine and turn until the outer bowl locks into place. Push the SMOOTHIE button. During the SMOOTHIE function, the ingredients will mix together and become very creamy.
3. Once the SMOOTHIE function has ended, turn the outer bowl and release it from the ninja CREAMi machine.
4. Scoop the smoothie into a tall glass.

Nutrition Info:

- InfoCalories 136,Protein 12g,Carbohydrate 20g,Fat 0.3g,Sodium 103mg.

Ice Cream Mix-ins Recipes

Sneaky Mint Chip Ice Cream

Servings:4
Cooking Time:x
Ingredients:

- 3 large egg yolks
- 1 tablespoon corn syrup
- ¼ cup granulated sugar
- ⅓ cup whole milk
- ¾ cup heavy (whipping) cream
- 1 cup packed fresh spinach
- ½ cup frozen peas, thawed
- 1 teaspoon mint extract
- ¼ cup semisweet chocolate chips

Directions:
1. Fill a large bowl with ice water and set it aside.
2. In a small saucepan, whisk together the egg yolks, corn syrup, and sugar until the mixture is fully combined and the sugar is dissolved. Do not do this over heat.
3. Whisk in the milk and heavy cream.
4. Place the pan over medium heat. Cook, stirring constantly with a rubber spatula, until the temperature reaches 165°F to 175°F on an instant-read thermometer.
5. Remove the pan from the heat and pour the base into a clean CREAMi Pint. Carefully place the container in the prepared ice water bath, making sure the water doesn't spill into the base.
6. Once the mixture has completely cooled, pour the base into a blender and add the spinach, peas, and mint extract. Blend on high for 30 seconds. Strain the base through a fine-mesh strainer back into the CREAMi Pint. Place the storage lid on the container and freeze for 24 hours.
7. Remove the pint from the freezer and take off the lid. Place the pint in the outer bowl of your Ninja CREAMi, install the Creamerizer Paddle in the outer bowl lid, and lock the lid assembly onto the outer bowl. Place the bowl assembly on the motor base, and twist the handle to the right to raise the platform and lock it in place. Select the Ice Cream function.
8. Once the machine has finished processing, remove the lid from the pint container. With a spoon, create a 1½-inch-wide hole that reaches the bottom of the pint. During this process, it is okay if your treat reaches above the Max Fill line. Add the chocolate chips to the hole in the pint, replace the lid, and select the Mix-In function.
9. Once the machine has finished processing, remove the ice cream from the pint. Serve immediately.

Lavender Cookies & Cream Ice Cream

Servings: 2
Cooking Time: 24 Hours And 20 Minutes
Ingredients:

- ½ cup heavy cream
- ½ tablespoon dried culinary lavender
- ¼ teaspoon kosher salt
- ½ cup whole milk
- ¼ cup sweetened condensed milk
- 2 drops purple food coloring
- ¼ cup crushed chocolate wafer cookies

Directions:
1. Whisk together the heavy cream, lavender, and salt in a medium saucepan.
2. Steep the mixture for 10 minutes over low heat, stirring every 2 minutes to prevent bubbling.
3. Using a fine-mesh strainer, drain the lavender from the heavy cream into a large mixing basin. Discard the lavender.
4. Combine the milk, sweetened condensed milk, and purple food coloring in a large mixing bowl. Whisk until the mixture is completely smooth.
5. Pour the base into an empty CREAMi Pint. Place the Pint into an ice bath. Once cooled, place the storage lid on the Pint and freeze for 24 hours.
6. Remove the Pint from the freezer and remove its lid. Place Pint in outer bowl, install Creamerizer Paddle in outer bowl lid, and lock the lid assembly onto the outer bowl. Select ICE CREAM.
7. When the process is done, create a 1½-inch wide hole that reaches the bottom of the Pint with a spoon. It's okay if your treat exceeds the max fill line. Add crushed wafer cookies to the hole and process again using the MIX-IN program.
8. When processing is complete, remove ice cream from Pint and serve immediately, topped with extra crumbled wafers if desired.

Nutrition Info:

- InfoCalories 180,Protein 3g,Carbohydrate 19g,Fat 16g,Sodium 60mg.

Vanilla Ice Cream With Chocolate Chips

Servings: 4
Cooking Time: 24 Hours And 5 Minutes
Ingredients:
- 1 tablespoon cream cheese, softened
- ⅓ cup granulated sugar
- 1 teaspoon vanilla extract
- ¾ cup heavy cream
- 1 cup whole milk
- ¼ cup mini chocolate chips, for mix-in

Directions:
1. Microwave the cream cheese for 10 seconds in a large microwave-safe bowl. With a rubber spatula, blend in the sugar and vanilla extract until the mixture resembles frosting, about 60 seconds.
2. Slowly whisk in the heavy cream and milk until smooth and the sugar has dissolved.
3. Pour the base into an empty CREAMi Pint. Place the storage lid on the Pint and freeze for 24 hours.
4. Remove the Pint from the freezer and remove the lid from the Pint. Place the Pint in the outer bowl, install the Creamerizer Paddle onto the outer bowl lid, and lock the lid assembly on the outer bowl. Select ICE CREAM.
5. With a spoon, create a 1½-inch wide hole that reaches the bottom of the Pint. During this process, it's okay for your treat to press above the max fill line. Add chocolate chips to the hole in the Pint and process again using the MIX-IN program.
6. When processing is complete, remove the ice cream from the Pint.

Nutrition Info:
- InfoCalories 160,Protein 2g,Carbohydrate 18g,Fat 8g,Sodium 46mg.

Chocolate-covered Coconut And Almond Ice Cream

Servings:4
Cooking Time:x
Ingredients:
- DAIRY-FREE, EGG-FREE, VEGAN
- PREP TIME: 5 minutes / Freeze time: 24 hours
- Functions: Ice Cream, Mix-In
- TOOLS NEEDED: Medium bowl, whisk, spoon
- 1 can full-fat unsweetened coconut milk
- ¼ cup unsweetened almond milk
- ½ cup organic sugar
- 1 teaspoon vanilla extract
- 2 tablespoons toasted almond halves
- 2 tablespoons vegan chocolate chips

Directions:
1. In a medium bowl, whisk together the coconut milk, almond milk, sugar, and vanilla until everything is incorporated and the sugar is dissolved.
2. Pour the base into a clean CREAMi Pint. Place the storage lid on the container and freeze for 24 hours.
3. Remove the pint from the freezer and take off the lid. Place the pint in the outer bowl of your Ninja CREAMi, install the Creamerizer Paddle in the outer bowl lid, and lock the lid assembly onto the outer bowl. Place the bowl assembly on the motor base, and twist the handle to the right to raise the platform and lock it in place. Select the Ice Cream function.
4. Once the machine has finished processing, remove the lid from the pint container. With a spoon, create a 1½-inch-wide hole that reaches the bottom of the pint. Add the almond halves and chocolate chips to the hole, then replace the lid and select the Mix-In function.
5. Once the machine has finished processing, remove the ice cream from the pint. Serve immediately.

Cookies & Cream Ice Cream

Servings: 2
Cooking Time: 24 Hours And 5 Minutes
Ingredients:

- ½ tablespoon cream cheese, softened
- ¼ cup granulated sugar
- ½ teaspoon vanilla extract
- ½ cup heavy cream
- ½ cup whole milk
- 1½ chocolate sandwich cookies, broken, for mix-in

Directions:

1. Microwave the cream cheese for 10 seconds in a large microwave-safe bowl. Combine the sugar and vanilla extract in a mixing bowl and whisk or scrape together until the mixture resembles frosting, about 60 seconds.
2. Slowly whisk in the heavy cream and milk until smooth and the sugar has dissolved.
3. Pour the base into an empty CREAMi Pint. Place storage lid on the Pint and freeze for 24 hours.
4. Remove the Pint from the freezer and remove the lid from the Pint. Place the Pint in the outer bowl, install Creamerizer Paddle onto the outer bowl lid, and lock the lid assembly on the outer bowl. Select ICE CREAM.
5. With a spoon, create a 1½-inch wide hole that reaches the bottom of the Pint. During this process, it's okay for your treat to go above the max fill line. Add the broken chocolate sandwich cookies to the hole and process again using the MIX-IN program.
6. When processing is complete, remove the ice cream from the Pint and serve immediately.

Nutrition Info:

- InfoCalories 140,Protein 2g,Carbohydrate 23g,Fat 4g,Sodium 86mg.

Snack Mix Ice Cream

Servings: 4
Cooking Time: 10 Seconds
Ingredients:

- 1 tablespoon cream cheese, softened
- ⅓ cup granulated sugar
- ½ teaspoon vanilla extract
- 1 cup whole milk
- ¾ cup heavy cream
- 2 tablespoons sugar cone pieces
- 1 tablespoon mini pretzels
- 1 tablespoon potato chips, crushed

Directions:

1. 1n a large microwave-safe bowl, add the cream cheese and microwave on High for about ten seconds.
2. Remove from the microwave and stir until smooth.
3. Add the sugar and vanilla extract and with a wire whisk, beat until the mixture looks like frosting.
4. Slowly add the milk and heavy cream and beat until well combined.
5. Transfer the mixture into an empty Ninja CREAMi pint container.
6. Cover the container with storage lid and freeze for 24 hours.
7. After 24 hours, remove the lid from container and arrange into the Outer Bowl of Ninja CREAMi.
8. Install the Creamerizer Paddle onto the lid of Outer Bowl.
9. Then rotate the lid clockwise to lock.
10. Press Power button to turn on the unit.
11. Then press Ice Cream button.
12. When the program is completed, with a spoon, create a 1½-inch wide hole in the center that reaches the bottom of the pint container.
13. Add the cone pieces, pretzels and potato chips into the hole and press Mix-In button.
14. When the program is completed, turn the Outer Bowl and release it from the machine.
15. Transfer the ice cream into serving bowls and serve immediately.

Nutrition Info:

- InfoCalories: 182,Fat: 4.3g,Carbohydrates: 32.8g,Protein: 3.6.

Coffee And Cookies Ice Cream

Servings:4
Cooking Time:x
Ingredients:

- 1 tablespoon cream cheese, at room temperature
- ⅓ cup granulated sugar
- 1 teaspoon vanilla extract
- 1 tablespoon instant espresso
- ¾ cup heavy (whipping) cream
- 1 cup whole milk
- ¼ cup crushed chocolate sandwich cookies

Directions:

1. In a large bowl, whisk together the cream cheese, sugar, and vanilla for about 1 minute, until the mixture looks like frosting.
2. Slowly whisk in the instant espresso, heavy cream, and milk until fully combined.
3. Pour the base into a clean CREAMi Pint. Place the lid on the container and freeze for 24 hours.
4. Remove the pint from the freezer and take off the lid. Place the pint in the outer bowl of your Ninja CREAMi, install the Creamerizer Paddle in the outer bowl lid, and lock the lid assembly onto the outer bowl. Place the bowl assembly on the motor base, and twist the handle to the right to raise the platform and lock it in place. Select the Ice Cream function.
5. Once the machine has finished processing, remove the lid from the pint container. With a spoon, create a 1½-inch-wide hole that reaches the bottom of the pint. Add the crushed cookies to the hole, replace the lid, and select the Mix-In function.
6. Once the machine has finished processing, remove the ice cream from the pint. Serve immediately.

Lavender Cookie Ice Cream

Servings: 4
Cooking Time: 10 Minutes
Ingredients:

- ¾ cup heavy cream
- 1 tablespoon dried culinary lavender
- 1/8 teaspoon salt
- ¾ cup whole milk
- ½ cup sweetened condensed milk
- 4 drops purple food coloring
- ⅓ cup chocolate wafer cookies, crushed

Directions:

1. In a medium saucepan, add heavy cream, lavender and salt and mix well.
2. Place the saucepan over low heat and steep, covered for about ten minutes, stirring after every two minutes.
3. Remove from the heat and through a fine-mesh strainer, strain the cream mixture into a large bowl.
4. Discard the lavender leaves.
5. In the bowl of cream mixture, add the milk, condensed milk and purple food coloring and beat until smooth.
6. Transfer the mixture into an empty Ninja CREAMi pint container.
7. Cover the container with storage lid and freeze for 24 hours.
8. After 24 hours, remove the lid from container and arrange into the Outer Bowl of Ninja CREAMi.
9. Install the Creamerizer Paddle onto the lid of Outer Bowl.
10. Then rotate the lid clockwise to lock.
11. Press Power button to turn on the unit.
12. Then press Ice Cream button.
13. When the program is completed, with a spoon, create a 1½-inch wide hole in the center that reaches the bottom of the pint container.
14. Add the crushed cookies the hole and press Mix-In button.
15. When the program is completed, turn the Outer Bowl and release it from the machine.
16. Transfer the ice cream into serving bowls and serve immediately.

Nutrition Info:

- InfoCalories: 229,Fat: 13.2g,Carbohydrates: 23.5g,Protein: 5.

Rum Raisin Ice Cream

Servings: 4
Cooking Time: 24 Hours And 23 Minutes
Ingredients:

- 3 large egg yolks
- ¼ cup dark brown sugar (or coconut sugar)
- 1 tablespoon light corn syrup
- ½ cup heavy cream
- 1 cup whole milk
- 1 teaspoon rum extract
- ⅓ cup raisins
- ¼ cup dark or spiced rum

Directions:

1. In a small saucepan, combine the egg yolks, sugar, and corn syrup. Whisk until everything is well mixed and the sugar has dissolved. Whisk together the heavy cream and milk until smooth.
2. Stir the mixture frequently with a whisk or a rubber spatula in a saucepan over medium-low heat. Using an instant-read thermometer, cook until the temperature hits 165°F–175°F.
3. Remove the base from heat, stir in the rum extract, then pour through a fine-mesh strainer into an empty CREAMi Pint. Place into an ice bath. Once cooled, place the storage lid on the Pint and freeze for 24 hours.
4. While the base is cooling, prepare the mix-in. Add the raisins and rum to a small bowl and microwave for 1 minute. Let cool, then drain the remaining rum. Cover and set aside.
5. Remove the Pint from the freezer and remove its lid. Place the Pint in the outer bowl, install the Creamerizer Paddle onto the outer bowl lid, and lock the lid assembly on the outer bowl. Select ICE CREAM.
6. With a spoon, create a 1½-inch wide hole that reaches the bottom of the Pint. Add the mixed raisins to the hole and process again using the MIX-IN program.
7. When processing is complete, remove the ice cream from the Pint.

Nutrition Info:

- InfoCalories 160,Protein 2g,Carbohydrate 18g,Fat 7g,Sodium 45mg.

Cookies And Coconut Ice Cream

Servings:4
Cooking Time:x
Ingredients:

- 1 can full-fat unsweetened coconut milk
- ½ cup organic sugar
- 1 teaspoon vanilla extract
- 4 chocolate sandwich cookies, crushed

Directions:

1. In a medium bowl, whisk together the coconut milk, sugar, and vanilla until well combined and the sugar is dissolved.
2. Pour the base into a clean CREAMi Pint. Place the storage lid on the container and freeze for 24 hours.
3. Remove the pint from the freezer and take off the lid. Place the pint in the outer bowl of your Ninja CREAMi, install the Creamerizer Paddle in the outer bowl lid, and lock the lid assembly onto the outer bowl. Place the bowl assembly on the motor base, and twist the handle to the right to raise the platform and lock it in place. Select the Ice Cream function.
4. Once the machine has finished processing, remove the lid from the pint container. With a spoon, create a 1½-inch-wide hole that reaches the bottom of the pint. During this process, it is okay if your treat reaches above the Max Fill line. Add the crushed cookies to the hole in the pint, replace the lid, and select the Mix-In function.
5. Once the machine has finished processing, remove the ice cream from the pint. Serve immediately with desired toppings.

Birthday Cake Ice Cream

Servings:4
Cooking Time:x
Ingredients:

- 5 large egg yolks
- ¼ cup corn syrup
- 2½ tablespoons granulated sugar
- ⅓ cup whole milk
- 1 cup heavy (whipping) cream
- 1½ tablespoons vanilla extract
- 3 tablespoons vanilla cake mix
- 2 tablespoons rainbow-colored sprinkles

Directions:

1. Fill a large bowl with ice water and set it aside.
2. In a small saucepan, whisk together the egg yolks, corn syrup, and sugar until the mixture is fully combined and the sugar is dissolved. Do not do this over heat.
3. Whisk in the milk, heavy cream, and vanilla.
4. Place the pan over medium heat. Cook, stirring constantly with a rubber spatula, until the temperature reaches 165°F to 175°F on an instant-read thermometer.
5. Remove the pan from the heat and pour the base through a fine-mesh strainer into a clean CREAMi Pint. Carefully place the container in the prepared ice water bath, making sure the water doesn't spill into the base.
6. Once the base has cooled, whisk in the vanilla cake mix until it is fully incorporated. Place the storage lid on the pint container and freeze for 24 hours.
7. Remove the pint from the freezer and take off the lid. Place the pint in the outer bowl of your Ninja CREAMi, install the Creamerizer Paddle in the outer bowl lid, and lock the lid assembly onto the outer bowl. Place the bowl assembly on the motor base, and twist the handle to the right to raise the platform and lock it in place. Select the Ice Cream function.
8. Once the machine has finished processing, remove the lid from the pint container. With a spoon, create a 1½-inch-wide hole that reaches the bottom of the pint. During this process, it is okay if your treat reaches above the Max Fill line. Add the rainbow sprinkles to the hole in the pint, replace the lid, and select the Mix-In function.
9. Once the machine has finished processing, remove the ice cream from the pint. Serve immediately.

Jelly & Peanut Butter Ice Cream

Servings: 4
Cooking Time: 5 Minutes
Ingredients:

- 3 tablespoons granulated sugar
- 4 large egg yolks
- 1 cup whole milk
- ⅓ cup heavy cream
- ¼ cup smooth peanut butter
- 3 tablespoons grape jelly
- ¼ cup honey roasted peanuts, chopped

Directions:

1. 1n a small saucepan, add the sugar and egg yolks and beat until sugar is dissolved.
2. Add the milk, heavy cream, peanut butter, and grape jelly to the saucepan and stir to combine.
3. Place saucepan over medium heat and cook until temperature reaches cook until temperature reaches to 165 -175° F, stirring continuously with a rubber spatula.
4. Remove from the heat and through a fine-mesh strainer, strain the mixture into an empty Ninja CREAMi pint container.
5. Place the container into ice bath to cool.
6. After cooling, cover the container with storage lid and freeze for 24 hours.
7. After 24 hours, remove the lid from container and arrange into the Outer Bowl of Ninja CREAMi.
8. Install the Creamerizer Paddle onto the lid of Outer Bowl.
9. Then rotate the lid clockwise to lock.
10. Press Power button to turn on the unit.
11. Then press ICE CREAM button.
12. When the program is completed, with a spoon, create a 1½-inch wide hole in the center that reaches the bottom of the pint container.
13. Add the peanuts into the hole and press Mix-In button.
14. When the program is completed, turn the Outer Bowl and release it from the machine.
15. Transfer the ice cream into serving bowls and serve immediately.

Nutrition Info:

- InfoCalories: 349,Fat: 23.1g,Carbohydrates: 27.5g,Protein: 11.5.

Cinnamon Cereal Milk Ice Cream

Servings:4
Cooking Time:x
Ingredients:

- 4 large egg yolks
- 1 tablespoon light corn syrup
- ¼ cup plus 1 tablespoon granulated sugar
- ⅓ cup whole milk
- 1 cup heavy (whipping) cream
- 1 teaspoon vanilla extract
- 3½ cups cinnamon square cereal, divided

Directions:

1. Fill a large bowl with ice water and set it aside.
2. In a small saucepan, whisk together the egg yolks, corn syrup, and sugar until the mixture is fully combined and the sugar is dissolved. Do not do this over heat.
3. Whisk in the milk, heavy cream, and vanilla.
4. Place the pan over medium heat. Cook, stirring constantly with a rubber spatula, until the temperature reaches 165°F to 175°F on an instant-read thermometer. Remove the pan from the heat and stir in 3 cups of cereal. Let steep for 20 minutes.
5. Remove the pan from the heat and pour the base through a fine-mesh strainer into a clean CREAMi Pint. Carefully place the container in the prepared ice water bath, making sure the water doesn't spill into the base.
6. Once the base has cooled, place the storage lid on the pint and freeze for 24 hours.
7. Remove the pint from the freezer and take off the lid. Place the pint in the outer bowl of your Ninja CREAMi, install the Creamerizer Paddle in the outer bowl lid, and lock the lid assembly onto the outer bowl. Place the bowl assembly on the motor base, and twist the handle to the right to raise the platform and lock it in place. Select the Ice Cream function.
8. Once the machine has finished processing, remove the lid from the pint container. With a spoon, create a 1½-inch-wide hole that reaches the bottom of the pint. During this process, it is okay if your treat reaches above the Max Fill line. Add the remaining ¼ cup of cereal to the hole in the pint, replace the lid, and select the Mix-In function.
9. Once processing is complete, remove the ice cream from the pint. Serve immediately.

Mint Cookies Ice Cream

Servings: 4
Cooking Time:x
Ingredients:

- ¾ cup coconut cream
- ¼ cup monk fruit sweetener with Erythritol
- 2 tablespoons agave nectar
- ½ teaspoon mint extract
- 5-6 drops green food coloring
- 1 cup oat milk
- 3 chocolate sandwich cookies, quartered

Directions:

1. 1n a large bowl, add the coconut cream and beat until smooth.
2. Add the sweetener, agave nectar, mint extract and food coloring and beat until sweetener is dissolved.
3. Add the oat milk and beat until well combined.
4. Transfer the mixture into an empty Ninja CREAMi pint container.
5. Cover the container with storage lid and freeze for 24 hours.
6. After 24 hours, remove the lid from container and arrange into the Outer Bowl of Ninja CREAMi.
7. Install the Creamerizer Paddle onto the lid of Outer Bowl.
8. Then rotate the lid clockwise to lock.
9. Press Power button to turn on the unit.
10. Then press Lite Ice Cream button.
11. When the program is completed, with a spoon, create a 1½-inch wide hole in the center that reaches the bottom of the pint container.
12. Add the cookie pieces into the hole and press Mix-In button.
13. When the program is completed, turn the Outer Bowl and release it from the machine.
14. Transfer the ice cream into serving bowls and serve immediately.

Nutrition Info:

- InfoCalories: 201,Fat: 12.8g,Carbohydrates: 21.9g,Protein: 2.4.

Triple-chocolate Ice Cream

Servings:4
Cooking Time:x
Ingredients:

- 4 large egg yolks
- ⅓ cup granulated sugar
- 1 tablespoon unsweetened cocoa powder
- 1 tablespoon hot fudge sauce
- ¾ cup heavy (whipping) cream
- ½ cup whole milk
- 1 teaspoon vanilla extract
- ¼ cup white chocolate chips

Directions:

1. Fill a large bowl with ice water and set it aside.
2. In a small saucepan, whisk together the egg yolks, sugar, and cocoa powder until the mixture is fully combined and the sugar is dissolved. Do not do this over heat.
3. Whisk in the hot fudge, heavy cream, milk, and vanilla.
4. Place the pan over medium heat. Cook, stirring constantly with a rubber spatula, until the temperature reaches 165°F to 175°F on an instant-read thermometer.
5. Remove the pan from the heat and pour the base through a fine-mesh strainer into a clean CREAMi Pint. Carefully place the container in the prepared ice water bath, making sure the water doesn't spill into the base.
6. Once the base has cooled, place the storage lid on the pint and freeze for 24 hours.
7. Remove the pint from the freezer and take off the lid. Place the pint in the outer bowl of your Ninja CREAMi, install the Creamerizer Paddle in the outer bowl lid, and lock the lid assembly onto the outer bowl. Place the bowl assembly on the motor base, and twist the handle to the right to raise the platform and lock it in place. Select the Ice Cream function.
8. Once the machine has finished processing, remove the lid from the pint container. With a spoon, create a 1½-inch-wide hole that reaches the bottom of the pint. During this process, it is okay if your treat reaches above the Max Fill line. Add the white chocolate chips to the hole in the pint, replace the lid, and select the Mix-In function.
9. Once the machine has finished processing, remove the ice cream from the pint. Serve immediately with desired toppings.

Bourbon-maple-walnut Ice Cream

Servings:4
Cooking Time:x
Ingredients:

- 4 large egg yolks
- ¼ cup maple syrup
- ¼ cup corn syrup
- 2 tablespoons bourbon
- ½ cup whole milk
- 1 cup heavy (whipping) cream
- ¼ cup toasted walnut halves

Directions:

1. Fill a large bowl with ice water and set it aside.
2. In a small saucepan, whisk together the egg yolks, maple syrup, corn syrup, and bourbon until the mixture is fully combined. Do not do this over heat.
3. Whisk in the milk and heavy cream.
4. Place the pan over medium heat. Cook, stirring constantly with a rubber spatula, until the temperature reaches 165°F to 175°F on an instant-read thermometer.
5. Remove the pan from the heat and pour the base into a clean CREAMi Pint. Carefully place the container in the prepared ice water bath, making sure the water doesn't spill into the base.
6. Once the base has cooled, place the storage lid on the pint and freeze for 24 hours.
7. Remove the pint from the freezer and take off the lid. Place the pint in the outer bowl of your Ninja CREAMi, install the Creamerizer Paddle in the outer bowl lid, and lock the lid assembly onto the outer bowl. Place the bowl assembly on the motor base, and twist the handle to the right to raise the platform and lock it in place. Select the Ice Cream function.
8. Once the machine has finished processing, remove the lid from the pint container. With a spoon, create a 1½-inch-wide hole that reaches the bottom of the pint. During this process, it is okay if your treat reaches above the Max Fill line. Add the toasted walnuts to the hole in the pint, replace the lid, and select the Mix-In function.
9. Once the machine has finished processing, remove the ice cream from the pint. Serve immediately.

Coffee Chip Ice Cream

Servings: 4
Cooking Time:x
Ingredients:

- ¾ cup heavy cream
- ¼ cup monk fruit sweetener with Erythritol
- ½ teaspoon stevia sweetener
- 1½ tablespoons instant coffee granules
- 1 cup unsweetened almond milk
- 1 teaspoon vanilla extract
- 3 tablespoons chocolate chips
- 1 tablespoon walnuts, chopped

Directions:

1. In a bowl, add the heavy cream and beat until smooth.
2. Add the remaining ingredients except for chocolate chips and walnuts and beat sweetener is dissolved.
3. Transfer the mixture into an empty Ninja CREAMi pint container.
4. Cover the container with storage lid and freeze for 24 hours.
5. After 24 hours, remove the lid from container and arrange into the Outer Bowl of Ninja CREAMi.
6. Install the Creamerizer Paddle onto the lid of Outer Bowl.
7. Then rotate the lid clockwise to lock.
8. Press Power button to turn on the unit.
9. Then press Lite Ice Cream button.
10. When the program is completed, with a spoon, create a 1½-inch wide hole in the center that reaches the bottom of the pint container.
11. Add the chocolate chips and walnuts into the hole and press Mix-In button.
12. When the program is completed, turn the Outer Bowl and release it from the machine.
13. Transfer the ice cream into serving bowls and serve immediately.

Nutrition Info:

- InfoCalories: 145,Fat: 12.7g,Carbohydrates: 6.1g,Protein: 1.8.

Rocky Road Ice Cream

Servings: 4
Cooking Time:x
Ingredients:

- 1 cup whole milk
- ½ cup frozen cauliflower florets, thawed
- ½ cup dark brown sugar
- 3 tablespoons dark cocoa powder
- 1 teaspoon chocolate extract
- ⅓ cup heavy cream
- 2 tablespoons almonds, sliced
- 2 tablespoons mini marshmallows
- 2 tablespoons mini chocolate chips

Directions:

1. 1n a high-speed blender, add milk, cauliflower, brown sugar, cocoa powder, and chocolate extract and pulse until smooth.
2. Transfer the mixture into an empty Ninja CREAMi pint container.
3. Add the heavy cream and stir until well combined.
4. Cover the container with storage lid and freeze for 24 hours.
5. After 24 hours, remove the lid from container and arrange into the Outer Bowl of Ninja CREAMi.
6. Install the Creamerizer Paddle onto the lid of Outer Bowl.
7. Then rotate the lid clockwise to lock.
8. Press Power button to turn on the unit.
9. Then press Ice Cream button.
10. When the program is completed, with a spoon, create a 1½-inch wide hole in the center that reaches the bottom of the pint container.
11. Add the almonds, marshmallows and chocolate chips into the hole and press Mix-In button.
12. When the program is completed, turn the Outer Bowl and release it from the machine.
13. Transfer the ice cream into serving bowls and serve immediately.

Nutrition Info:

- InfoCalories: 202,Fat: 9.3g,Carbohydrates: 28.7g,Protein: 4.2.

Fruity Cereal Ice Cream

Servings: 2
Cooking Time: 24 Hours And 30 Minutes
Ingredients:

- ¾ cup whole milk
- 1 cup fruity cereal, divided
- 1 tablespoon Philadelphia cream cheese, softened
- ¼ cup granulated sugar
- 1 teaspoon vanilla extract
- ½ cup heavy cream

Directions:

1. In a large mixing bowl, combine ½ cup of the fruity cereal and the milk. Allow the mixture to settle for 15–30 minutes, stirring occasionally to infuse the milk with the fruity taste.
2. Microwave the Philadelphia cream cheese for 10 seconds in a second large microwave-safe dish. Combine the sugar and vanilla extract in a mixing bowl with a whisk or rubber spatula until the mixture resembles frosting, about 60 seconds.
3. After 15 to 30 minutes, sift the milk and cereal into the bowl with the sugar mixture using a fine-mesh filter. To release extra milk, press on the cereal with a spoon, then discard it. Mix in the heavy cream until everything is thoroughly mixed.
4. Pour the mixture into an empty ninja CREAMi Pint container. Add the strawberries to the Pint, making sure not to go over the max fill line, and freeze for 24 hours.
5. After 24 hours, remove the Pint from the freezer. Remove the lid.
6. Place the Ninja CREAMi Pint into the outer bowl. Place the outer bowl with the Pint in it into the ninja CREAMi machine and turn until the outer bowl locks into place. Push the ICE CREAM button. During the ICE CREAM function, the ice cream will mix together and become very creamy.
7. Use a spoon to create a 1½-inch wide hole that reaches the bottom of the Pint. Add the remaining ½ cup of fruity cereal to the hole and process again using the mix-in. When processing is complete, remove the ice cream from the Pint.

Nutrition Info:

- InfoCalories 140,Protein 0.5g,Carbohydrate 25g,Fat 2g,Sodium 46mg.

Chocolate Brownie Ice Cream

Servings: 4
Cooking Time:x
Ingredients:

- 1 tablespoon cream cheese, softened
- ⅓ cup granulated sugar
- 1 teaspoon vanilla extract
- 2 tablespoons cocoa powder
- 1 cup whole milk
- ¾ cup heavy cream
- 2 tablespoons mini chocolate chips
- 2 tablespoons brownie chunks

Directions:

1. 1n a large microwave-safe bowl, add the cream cheese and microwave on High for about ten seconds.
2. Remove from the microwave and stir until smooth.
3. Add the sugar and almond extract and with a wire whisk, beat until the mixture looks like frosting.
4. Slowly add the milk and heavy cream and beat until well combined.
5. Transfer the mixture into an empty Ninja CREAMi pint container.
6. Cover the container with storage lid and freeze for 24 hours.
7. After 24 hours, remove the lid from container and arrange into the Outer Bowl of Ninja CREAMi.
8. Install the Creamerizer Paddle onto the lid of Outer Bowl.
9. Then rotate the lid clockwise to lock.
10. Press Power button to turn on the unit.
11. Then press Ice Cream button.
12. When the program is completed, with a spoon, create a 1½-inch wide hole in the center that reaches the bottom of the pint container.
13. Add the chocolate chunks and brownie pieces into the hole and press Mix-In button.
14. When the program is completed, turn the Outer Bowl and release it from the machine.
15. Transfer the ice cream into serving bowls and serve immediately.

Nutrition Info:

- InfoCalories: 232,Fat: 13.7g,Carbohydrates: 25.9g,Protein: 3.6.

Grasshopper Ice Cream

Servings: 4
Cooking Time:x
Ingredients:

- ½ cup frozen spinach, thawed and squeezed dry
- 1 cup whole milk
- ½ cup granulated sugar
- 1 teaspoon mint extract
- 3-5 drops green food coloring
- ⅓ cup heavy cream
- ¼ cup chocolate chunks, chopped
- ¼ cup brownie, cut into 1-inch pieces

Directions:

1. In a high-speed blender, add the spinach, milk, sugar, mint extract and food coloring and pulse until mixture smooth.
2. Transfer the mixture into an empty Ninja CREAMi pint container.
3. Add the heavy cream and stir until well combined.
4. Cover the container with storage lid and freeze for 24 hours.
5. After 24 hours, remove the lid from container and arrange into the Outer Bowl of Ninja CREAMi.
6. Install the Creamerizer Paddle onto the lid of Outer Bowl.
7. Then rotate the lid clockwise to lock.
8. Press Power button to turn on the unit.
9. Then press Ice Cream button.
10. When the program is completed, with a spoon, create a 1½-inch wide hole in the center that reaches the bottom of the pint container.
11. Add the chocolate chunks and brownie pieces into the hole and press Mix-In button.
12. When the program is completed, turn the Outer Bowl and release it from the machine.
13. Transfer the ice cream into serving bowls and serve immediately.

Nutrition Info:

- InfoCalories: 243,Fat: 10.1g,Carbohydrates: 36.7g,Protein: 3.4.

Sweet Potato Pie Ice Cream

Servings:4
Cooking Time:x
Ingredients:

- 1 cup canned pureed sweet potato
- 1 tablespoon corn syrup
- ¼ cup plus 1 tablespoon light brown sugar
- 1 teaspoon vanilla extract
- 1 teaspoon cinnamon
- ¾ cup heavy (whipping) cream
- ¼ cup mini marshmallows

Directions:

1. Combine the sweet potato puree, corn syrup, brown sugar, vanilla, and cinnamon in a blender. Blend on high until smooth.
2. Pour the base into a clean CREAMi Pint. Whisk in the heavy cream until combined. Place the storage lid on the container and freeze for 24 hours.
3. Remove the pint from the freezer and take off the lid. Place the pint in the outer bowl of your Ninja CREAMi, install the Creamerizer Paddle in the outer bowl lid, and lock the lid assembly onto the outer bowl. Place the bowl assembly on the motor base, and twist the handle to the right to raise the platform and lock it in place. Select the Ice Cream function.
4. Once the machine has finished processing, remove the lid from the pint container. With a spoon, create a 1½-inch-wide hole that reaches the bottom of the pint. During this process, it is okay if your treat reaches above the Max Fill line. Add the marshmallows to the hole in the pint, replace the lid, and select the Mix-In function.
5. Once the machine has finished processing, remove the ice cream from the pint. Serve immediately with desired toppings.

Pistachio Ice Cream

Servings: 4
Cooking Time:x
Ingredients:
- 1 tablespoon cream cheese, softened
- ⅓ cup granulated sugar
- 1 teaspoon almond extract
- 1 cup whole milk
- ¾ cup heavy cream
- ¼ cup pistachios, shells removed and chopped

Directions:
1. 1n a large microwave-safe bowl, add the cream cheese and microwave on High for about ten seconds.
2. Remove from the microwave and stir until smooth.
3. Add the sugar and almond extract and with a wire whisk, beat until the mixture looks like frosting.
4. Slowly add the milk and heavy cream and beat until well combined.
5. Transfer the mixture into an empty Ninja CREAMi pint container.
6. Cover the container with storage lid and freeze for 24 hours.
7. After 24 hours, remove the lid from container and arrange into the Outer Bowl of Ninja CREAMi.
8. Install the Creamerizer Paddle onto the lid of Outer Bowl.
9. Then rotate the lid clockwise to lock.
10. Press Power button to turn on the unit.
11. Then press Ice Cream button.
12. When the program is completed, with a spoon, create a 1½-inch wide hole in the center that reaches the bottom of the pint container.
13. Add the pistachios into the hole and press Mix-In button.
14. When the program is completed, turn the Outer Bowl and release it from the machine.
15. Transfer the ice cream into serving bowls and serve immediately.

Nutrition Info:
- InfoCalories: 208,Fat: 12.9g,Carbohydrates: 21.3g,Protein: 3.4.

Coconut Mint Chip Ice Cream

Servings:4
Cooking Time:x
Ingredients:
- 1 can full-fat unsweetened coconut milk
- ½ cup organic sugar
- ½ teaspoon mint extract
- ¼ cup mini vegan chocolate chips

Directions:
1. In a medium bowl, whisk together the coconut milk, sugar, and mint extract until everything is well combined and the sugar is dissolved.
2. Pour the base into a clean CREAMi Pint. Place the storage lid on the container and freeze for 24 hours.
3. Remove the pint from the freezer and take off the lid. Place the pint in the outer bowl of your Ninja CREAMi, install the Creamerizer Paddle in the outer bowl lid, and lock the lid assembly onto the outer bowl. Place the bowl assembly on the motor base, and twist the handle to the right to raise the platform and lock it in place. Select the Ice Cream function.
4. Once the machine has finished processing, remove the lid from the pint container. With a spoon, create a 1½-inch-wide hole that reaches the bottom of the pint. During this process, it is okay if your treat reaches above the Max Fill line. Add the mini chocolate chips to the hole in the pint, replace the lid, and select the Mix-In function.
5. Once the machine has finished processing, remove the ice cream from the pint. Serve immediately with desired toppings.

Lite Chocolate Cookie Ice Cream

Servings: 2

Cooking Time: 24 Hours And 5 Minutes

Ingredients:

- 1 tablespoon cream cheese, at room temperature
- 2 tablespoons unsweetened cocoa powder
- ½ teaspoon stevia sweetener
- 3 tablespoons raw agave nectar
- 1 teaspoon vanilla extract
- ¾ cup heavy cream
- 1 cup whole milk
- ¼ cup crushed reduced-fat sugar cookies

Directions:

1. Place the cream cheese in a large microwave-safe bowl and heat on high for 10 seconds.
2. Mix in the cocoa powder, stevia, agave, and vanilla. Microwave for 60 seconds more, or until the mixture resembles frosting.
3. Slowly whisk in the heavy cream and milk until the sugar has dissolved and the mixture is thoroughly mixed.
4. Pour the base into a clean CREAMi Pint. Place the storage lid on the container and freeze for 24 hours.
5. Remove the Pint from the freezer and take off the lid. Place the Pint in the outer bowl of your Ninja CREAMi, install the Creamerizer Paddle in the outer bowl lid, and lock the lid assembly onto the outer bowl. Place the bowl assembly on the motor base, and twist the handle to the right to raise the platform and lock it in place. Select the LITE ICE CREAM function.
6. Once the machine has finished processing, remove the lid. With a spoon, create a 1½-inch-wide hole that reaches the bottom of the Pint. During this process, it's okay if your treat goes above the max fill line. Add the crushed cookies to the hole in the Pint. Replace the Pint lid and select the MIX-IN function.
7. Once the machine has finished processing, remove the ice cream from the Pint.

Nutrition Info:

- InfoCalories 150,Protein 5g,Carbohydrate 25g,Fat 4g,Sodium 65mg.

Milkshake Recipes

Healthy Strawberry Shake

Servings: 1
Cooking Time: 10 Minutes
Ingredients:

- 1 cup milk
- 1 tablespoon honey
- ½ teaspoon vanilla extract
- ½ cup frozen strawberries

Directions:

1. Add the milk, honey, vanilla extract, and strawberries into an empty CREAMi Pint.
2. Place Pint in outer bowl, install Creamerizer Paddle onto outer bowl lid and lock the lid assembly on the outer bowl. Place the bowl assembly on the motor base and crank the lever to elevate and secure the platform in place.
3. Select MILKSHAKE.
4. Remove the milkshake from the Pint after the processing is finished.

Nutrition Info:

- InfoCalories 186,Protein 8.4g,Carbohydrate 27g,Fat 5g,Sodium 102mg.

Dulce De Leche Milkshake

Servings: 2
Cooking Time: 5 Minutes
Ingredients:

- 1 cup vanilla or coffee ice cream
- ½ cup milk
- 2 tablespoons sweetened condensed milk
- ¼ teaspoon salt

Directions:

1. Place all ingredients into an empty CREAMi Pint.
2. Place Pint in outer bowl, install Creamerizer Paddle onto outer bowl lid and lock the lid assembly on the outer bowl. Place the bowl assembly on the motor base and crank the lever to elevate and secure the platform in place.
3. Choose the MILKSHAKE option.
4. Remove the milkshake from the Pint after the function is finished.

Nutrition Info:

- InfoCalories 276,Protein 7g,Carbohydrate 48g,Fat 6g,Sodium 530mg.

Pecan Milkshake

Servings: 2
Cooking Time:x
Ingredients:

- 1½ cups vanilla ice cream
- ½ cup unsweetened soy milk
- 2 tablespoons maple syrup
- ¼ cup pecans, chopped
- 1 teaspoon ground cinnamon
- Pinch of salt

Directions:

1. In an empty Ninja CREAMi pint container, place ice cream followed by soy milk, maple syrup, pecans, cinnamon and salt.
2. Arrange the container into the Outer Bowl of Ninja CREAMi.
3. Install the Creamerizer Paddle onto the lid of Outer Bowl.
4. Then rotate the lid clockwise to lock.
5. Press Power button to turn on the unit.
6. Then press Milkshake button.
7. When the program is completed, turn the Outer Bowl and release it from the machine.
8. Transfer the shake into serving glasses and serve immediately.

Nutrition Info:

- InfoCalories: 309,Fat: 18.5g,Carbohydrates: 32.6g,Protein: 5.6.

Mixed Berries Milkshake

Servings: 2
Cooking Time:x
Ingredients:
- 1½ cups vanilla ice cream
- ½ cup milk
- ½ cup fresh mixed berries

Directions:
1. In an empty Ninja CREAMi pint container, place ice cream followed by milk and berries.
2. Arrange the container into the outer bowl of Ninja CREAMi.
3. Install the Creamerizer Paddle onto the lid of Outer Bowl.
4. Then rotate the lid clockwise to lock.
5. Press Power button to turn on the unit.
6. Then press Milkshake button.
7. When the program is completed, turn the Outer Bowl and release it from the machine.
8. Transfer the shake into serving glasses and serve immediately.

Nutrition Info:
- InfoCalories: 153,Fat: 6.6g,Carbohydrates: 19.3g,Protein: 4.

Caramel Cone Milkshake

Servings:4
Cooking Time:x
Ingredients:
- 1½ cups vanilla ice cream
- ½ cup whole milk
- 3 tablespoons caramel sauce
- 1 waffle cone, crushed or finely chopped

Directions:
1. Combine the vanilla ice cream, milk, and caramel sauce in a clean CREAMi Pint.
2. With a spoon, create a 1½-inch-wide hole that reaches the bottom of the pint. During this process, it is okay if your treat reaches above the Max Fill line. Add the crushed waffle cone to the hole in the pint.
3. Place the pint in the outer bowl of your Ninja CREAMi, install the Creamerizer Paddle in the outer bowl lid, and lock the lid assembly onto the outer bowl. Place the bowl assembly on the motor base, and twist the handle to the right to raise the platform and lock it in place. Select the Milkshake function.
4. Once the machine has finished processing, remove the milkshake from the pint. Serve immediately.

Orange Milkshake

Servings: 1
Cooking Time: 5 Minutes
Ingredients:
- 1 cup orange juice
- 2 scoops vanilla ice cream
- ½ cup milk
- 2 teaspoons white sugar

Directions:
1. Place orange juice, ice cream, milk, and sugar in an empty CREAMi Pint.
2. Place Pint in outer bowl, install Creamerizer Paddle onto outer bowl lid and lock the lid assembly on the outer bowl. Place the bowl assembly on the motor base and crank the lever to elevate and secure the platform in place.
3. Select MILKSHAKE.
4. Remove the milkshake from the Pint after the processing is finished.

Nutrition Info:
- InfoCalories 346,Protein 8g,Carbohydrate 62g,Fat 7.8g,Sodium 87.3mg.

Mocha Banana Milkshake

Servings: 2
Cooking Time:x
Ingredients:

- 1½ C. chocolate ice cream
- ½ C. cashew milk
- ½ C. ripe banana, peeled and cut into ½-inch pieces
- 1 tbsp. instant coffee powder

Directions:

1. In an empty Ninja CREAMi pint container, place ice cream, followed by milk, banana and coffee powder.
2. Arrange the container into the outer bowl of Ninja CREAMi.
3. Install the "Creamerizer Paddle" onto the lid of outer bowl.
4. Then rotate the lid clockwise to lock.
5. Press "Power" button to turn on the unit.
6. Then press "MILKSHAKE" button.
7. When the program is completed, turn the outer bowl and release it from the machine.
8. Transfer the shake into serving glasses and serve immediately.

Nutrition Info:

- InfoCalories: 142,Carbohydrates: 20.8g,Protein: 3.2g,Fat: 5.9g,Sodium: 84m.

Lite Raspberry Ice Cream

Servings:4
Cooking Time:x
Ingredients:

- 1½ cups fresh raspberries
- 1 teaspoon freshly squeezed lemon juice
- ¼ cup stevia–cane sugar sweetener blend
- 1 teaspoon raw agave nectar
- 1 cup heavy cream

Directions:

1. In a blender, combine the raspberries and lemon juice; puree until smooth.
2. Pour the raspberry and lemon mixture into a large bowl, add the stevia blend and agave nectar, and mix until well combined. Stir in the heavy cream.
3. Pour the base into a clean CREAMi Pint. Place the storage lid on the container and freeze for 24 hours.
4. Remove the pint from the freezer and take off the lid. Place the pint in the outer bowl of your Ninja CREAMi, install the Creamerizer Paddle in the outer bowl lid, and lock the lid assembly onto the outer bowl. Place the bowl assembly on the motor base, and twist the handle to the right to raise the platform and lock it in place. Select the Lite Ice Cream function.
5. Once the machine has finished processing, remove the ice cream from the pint. Serve immediately.

Cookie Milkshake

Servings: 1
Cooking Time: 5 Minutes
Ingredients:

- 1 cup whole milk
- ½ cup amaretto-flavored coffee creamer
- ¼ cup amaretto liqueur
- 1 tablespoon agave nectar
- ¼ cup chopped chocolate chip cookies

Directions:

1. In a clean CREAMi Pint, combine the milk, coffee creamer, amaretto liqueur, and agave nectar in a large mixing bowl. Stir everything together thoroughly. Freeze for 24 hours with the storage cover on the container.
2. Remove the Pint from the freezer and take off the lid. Place the Pint in the outer bowl of your Ninja CREAMi, install the Creamerizer Paddle in the outer bowl lid, and lock the lid assembly onto the outer bowl. To raise the platform and secure it in position, set the bowl assembly on the motor base and twist the handle to the right.
3. Select MILKSHAKE.
4. Remove the cover when the machine has finished processing. Create a 1½-inch-wide hole in the bottom of the Pint using a spoon. Add the chopped cookies to the hole in the Pint, replace the lid, and select MIX-IN.

Nutrition Info:

- InfoCalories 356,Protein 16g,Carbohydrate 58g,Fat 7g,Sodium 400mg.

Dairy-free Strawberry Milkshake

Servings:2
Cooking Time:x
Ingredients:

- 1½ cups Coconut-Vanilla Ice Cream
- ½ cup oat milk
- 3 fresh strawberries

Directions:

1. Combine the ice cream, oat milk, and strawberries in a clean CREAMi Pint.
2. Place the pint in the outer bowl of your Ninja CREAMi, install the Creamerizer Paddle in the outer bowl lid, and lock the lid assembly onto the outer bowl. Place the bowl assembly on the motor base, and twist the handle to the right to raise the platform and lock it in place. Select the Milkshake function.
3. Once the machine has finished processing, remove the milkshake from the pint. Serve immediately.

Chocolate Ice Cream Milkshake

Servings: 1
Cooking Time:x
Ingredients:

- 1½ cups chocolate ice cream
- ½ cup whole milk

Directions:

1. In an empty Ninja CREAMi pint container, place ice cream, followed by milk.
2. Arrange the container into the Outer Bowl of Ninja CREAMi.
3. Install the Creamerizer Paddle onto the lid of Outer Bowl.
4. Then rotate the lid clockwise to lock.
5. Press Power button to turn on the unit.
6. Then press Milkshake button.
7. When the program is completed, turn the Outer Bowl and release it from the machine.
8. Transfer the shake into a serving glass and serve immediately.

Nutrition Info:

- InfoCalories: 279,Fat: 14.5g,Carbohydrates: 29.5g,Protein: 7.4.

Chocolate Protein Milkshake

Servings: 2
Cooking Time:x
Ingredients:

- 1 C. frozen chocolate yogurt
- 1 scoop chocolate whey protein powder
- 1 C. whole milk

Directions:

1. In an empty Ninja CREAMi pint container, place yogurt, followed by protein powder and milk.
2. Arrange the container into the outer bowl of Ninja CREAMi.
3. Install the "Creamerizer Paddle" onto the lid of outer bowl.
4. Then rotate the lid clockwise to lock.
5. Press "Power" button to turn on the unit.
6. Then press "MILKSHAKE" button.
7. When the program is completed, turn the outer bowl and release it from the machine.
8. Transfer the shake into serving glasses and serve immediately.

Nutrition Info:

- InfoCalories: 242,Carbohydrates: 30.7g,Protein: 18.6g,Fat: 4.8g,Sodium: 104m.

Vanilla Milkshake

Servings: 2
Cooking Time:x
Ingredients:

- 2 cups French vanilla coffee creamer
- 1 tablespoon agave nectar
- 2 ounces vodka
- 1 tablespoon rainbow sprinkles

Directions:

1. In an empty Ninja CREAMi pint container, place all ingredients and mix well.
2. Cover the container with storage lid and freeze for 24 hours.
3. After 24 hours, remove the lid from container and arrange into the Outer Bowl of Ninja CREAMi.
4. Install the Creamerizer Paddle onto the lid of Outer Bowl.
5. Then rotate the lid clockwise to lock.
6. Press Power button to turn on the unit.
7. Then press Milkshake button.
8. When the program is completed, turn the Outer Bowl and release it from the machine.
9. Transfer the shake into serving glasses and serve immediately.

Nutrition Info:

- InfoCalories: 563,Fat: 46.3g,Carbohydrates: 16.8g,Protein: 6.5.

Lemon Cookie Milkshake

Servings: 2
Cooking Time:x
Ingredients:

- 1½ cups vanilla ice cream
- 3 lemon cream sandwich cookies
- ¼ cup milk

Directions:

1. In an empty Ninja CREAMi pint container, place ice cream followed by cookies and milk.
2. Arrange the container into the Outer Bowl of Ninja CREAMi.
3. Install the Creamerizer Paddle onto the lid of Outer Bowl.
4. Then rotate the lid clockwise to lock.
5. Press Power button to turn on the unit.
6. Then press Milkshake button.
7. When the program is completed, turn the Outer Bowl and release it from the machine.
8. Transfer the shake into serving glasses and serve immediately.

Nutrition Info:

- InfoCalories: 222,Fat: 10g,Carbohydrates: 29.1g,Protein: 3.8.

Baileys Milkshake

Servings: 1
Cooking Time: 5 Minutes
Ingredients:

- 1 scoop vanilla ice cream
- 1 scoop chocolate ice cream
- 1 tablespoon chocolate sauce
- 1 tablespoon caramel sauce
- 2 fluid ounces Baileys Irish Cream
- 1 cup whole milk

Directions:

1. Place all ingredients into an empty CREAMi Pint.
2. Place Pint in outer bowl, install Creamerizer Paddle onto outer bowl lid and lock the lid assembly on the outer bowl. Place the bowl assembly on the motor base and crank the lever to elevate and secure the platform in place.
3. Choose the MILKSHAKE option.
4. Remove the milkshake from the Pint after the processing is finished.

Nutrition Info:

- InfoCalories 718,Protein 18g,Carbohydrate 85g,Fat 22g,Sodium 369mg.

Lime Sherbet Milkshake

Servings: 1
Cooking Time:x
Ingredients:
- 1½ C. rainbow sherbet
- ½ C. lime seltzer

Directions:
1. In an empty Ninja CREAMi pint container, place sherbet and top with lime seltzer.
2. Arrange the container into the outer bowl of Ninja CREAMi.
3. Install the "Creamerizer Paddle" onto the lid of outer bowl.
4. Then rotate the lid clockwise to lock.
5. Press "Power" button to turn on the unit.
6. Then press "MILKSHAKE" button.
7. When the program is completed, turn the outer bowl and release it from the machine.
8. Transfer the shake into a serving glass and serve immediately.

Nutrition Info:
- InfoCalories: 195,Carbohydrates: 40.5g,Protein: 1.5g,Fat: 2.3g,Sodium: 94m.

Chocolate–peanut Butter Milkshake

Servings:2
Cooking Time:x
Ingredients:
- 1½ cups chocolate ice cream
- ½ cup whole milk
- ¼ cup mini peanut butter cups

Directions:
1. Combine the chocolate ice cream and milk in a clean CREAMi Pint.
2. Use a spoon to create a 1½-inch-wide hole that goes all the way to the bottom of the pint. Pour the mini peanut butter cups into the hole.
3. Place the pint in the outer bowl of your Ninja CREAMi, install the Creamerizer Paddle in the outer bowl lid, and lock the lid assembly onto the outer bowl. Place the bowl assembly on the motor base, and twist the handle to the right to raise the platform and lock it in place. Select the Milkshake function.
4. Once the machine has finished processing, remove the milkshake from the pint. Serve immediately.

Cacao Mint Milkshake

Servings: 2
Cooking Time:x
Ingredients:
- 1½ cups vanilla ice cream
- ½ cup canned full-fat coconut milk
- 1 teaspoon matcha powder
- ¼ cup cacao nibs
- 1 teaspoon peppermint extract

Directions:
1. In an empty Ninja CREAMi pint container, place ice cream followed by coconut milk, matcha powder, cacao nibs and peppermint extract.
2. Arrange the container into the Outer Bowl of Ninja CREAMi.
3. Install the Creamerizer Paddle onto the lid of Outer Bowl.
4. Then rotate the lid clockwise to lock.
5. Press Power button to turn on the unit.
6. Then press Milkshake button.
7. When the program is completed, turn the Outer Bowl and release it from the machine.
8. Transfer the shake into serving glasses and serve immediately.

Nutrition Info:
- InfoCalories: 363,Fat: 26.2g,Carbohydrates: 26.8g,Protein: 5.4.

Chocolate Ginger Milkshake

Servings: 2
Cooking Time:x
Ingredients:
- 1½ C. chocolate ice cream
- ½ C. oat milk
- 1 tsp. ground ginger
- ¼ C. chocolate, grated

Directions:
1. In an empty Ninja CREAMi pint container, place the ice cream.
2. With a spoon, create a 1½-inch wide hole in the center that reaches the bottom of the pint container.
3. Add the remaining ingredients into the hole.
4. Arrange the container into the outer bowl of Ninja CREAMi.
5. Install the "Creamerizer Paddle" onto the lid of outer bowl.
6. Then rotate the lid clockwise to lock.
7. Press "Power" button to turn on the unit.
8. Then press "MILKSHAKE" button.
9. When the program is completed, turn the outer bowl and release it from the machine.
10. Transfer the shake into serving glasses and serve immediately.

Nutrition Info:
- InfoCalories: 251,Carbohydrates: 31.1g,Protein: 4.4g,Fat: 12.2g,Sodium: 83m.

Coffee Vodka Milkshake

Servings: 2
Cooking Time:x
Ingredients:
- 2 C. vanilla ice cream
- 2 tbsp. coffee liqueur
- 2 tbsp. vodka

Directions:
1. In an empty Ninja CREAMi pint container, place ice cream, followed by coffee liqueur and vodka.
2. Arrange the container into the outer bowl of Ninja CREAMi.
3. Install the "Creamerizer Paddle" onto the lid of outer bowl.
4. Then rotate the lid clockwise to lock.
5. Press "Power" button to turn on the unit.
6. Then press "MILKSHAKE" button.
7. When the program is completed, turn the outer bowl and release it from the machine.
8. Transfer the shake into serving glasses and serve immediately.

Nutrition Info:
- InfoCalories: 226,Carbohydrates: 24.1g,Protein: 2.3g,Fat: 7.1g,Sodium: 144m.

Cacao Matcha Milkshake

Servings: 2
Cooking Time:x

Ingredients:

- 1½ C. vanilla ice cream
- ½ C. canned full-fat coconut milk
- 1 tsp. matcha powder
- ¼ C. cacao nibs
- ¾ tsp. peppermint extract
- ¼ tsp. vanilla extract

Directions:

1. In an empty Ninja CREAMi pint container, place ice cream, followed by coconut milk, matcha powder, cacao nibs and peppermint extract.
2. Arrange the container into the outer bowl of Ninja CREAMi.
3. Install the "Creamerizer Paddle" onto the lid of outer bowl.
4. Then rotate the lid clockwise to lock.
5. Press "Power" button to turn on the unit.
6. Then press "MILKSHAKE" button.
7. When the program is completed, turn the outer bowl and release it from the machine.
8. Transfer the shake into serving glasses and serve immediately.

Nutrition Info:

- InfoCalories: 363,Carbohydrates: 26.8g,Protein: 5.4g,Fat: 21.6g,Sodium: 120m.

Cashew Butter Milkshake

Servings: 2
Cooking Time:x

Ingredients:

- 1½ cups vanilla ice cream
- ½ cup canned cashew milk
- ¼ cup cashew butter

Directions:

1. In an empty Ninja CREAMi pint container, place the ice cream.
2. With a spoon, create a 1½-inch wide hole in the center that reaches the bottom of the pint container.
3. Add the remaining ingredients into the hole.
4. Arrange the container into the Outer Bowl of Ninja CREAMi.
5. Install the Creamerizer Paddle onto the lid of Outer Bowl.
6. Then rotate the lid clockwise to lock.
7. Press Power button to turn on the unit.
8. Then press Milkshake button.
9. When the program is completed, turn the Outer Bowl and release it from the machine.
10. Transfer the shake into serving glasses and serve immediately.

Nutrition Info:

- InfoCalories: 297,Fat: 21.6g,Carbohydrates: 21.1g,Protein: 7.4.

Chocolate-hazelnut Milkshake

Servings:4
Cooking Time:x
Ingredients:

- 2 tablespoons granulated sugar
- 2 tablespoons unsweetened cocoa powder
- ½ cup whole milk
- 1 cup hazelnut-flavored coffee creamer

Directions:

1. In a large bowl, whisk together the sugar, cocoa powder, milk, and coffee creamer until the sugar is fully dissolved.
2. Pour the base into a clean CREAMi Pint. Place the storage lid on the container and freeze for 24 hours.
3. Remove the pint from the freezer and take off the lid. Place the pint in the outer bowl of your Ninja CREAMi, install the Creamerizer Paddle in the outer bowl lid, and lock the lid assembly onto the outer bowl. Place the bowl assembly on the motor base, and twist the handle to the right to raise the platform and lock it in place. Select the Milkshake function.
4. Once the machine has finished processing, remove the milkshake from the pint. Serve immediately.

Amaretto Cookies Milkshake

Servings: 2
Cooking Time:x
Ingredients:

- 1 C. whole milk
- ½ C. amaretto-flavored coffee creamer
- ¼ C. amaretto liqueur
- 1 tbsp. agave nectar
- ¼ C. chocolate chip cookies, chopped

Directions:

1. In an empty Ninja CREAMi pint container, place all ingredients except for cookies and stir to combine.
2. Cover the container with the storage lid and freeze for 24 hours.
3. After 24 hours, remove the lid from container and arrange into the outer bowl of Ninja CREAMi.
4. Install the "Creamerizer Paddle" onto the lid of outer bowl.
5. Then rotate the lid clockwise to lock.
6. Press "Power" button to turn on the unit.
7. Then press "MILKSHAKE" button.
8. When the program is completed, with a spoon, create a 1½-inch wide hole in the center that reaches the bottom of the pint container.
9. Add the chopped cookies into the hole and press "MIX-IN" button.
10. When the program is completed, turn the outer bowl and release it from the machine.
11. Transfer the shake into serving glasses and serve immediately.

Nutrition Info:

- InfoCalories: 371,Carbohydrates: 25.9g,Protein: 6.5g,Fat: 17.6g,Sodium: 294m.

Mocha Milkshake

Servings: 2
Cooking Time:x
Ingredients:

- 1½ cups chocolate ice cream
- ½ cup cashew milk
- ½ cup ripe banana, peeled and cut into ½-inch pieces
- 1 tablespoon instant coffee powder

Directions:

1. In an empty Ninja CREAMi pint container, place ice cream followed by milk, banana and coffee powder.
2. Arrange the container into the Outer Bowl of Ninja CREAMi.
3. Install the Creamerizer Paddle onto the lid of Outer Bowl.
4. Then rotate the lid clockwise to lock.
5. Press Power button to turn on the unit.
6. Then press Milkshake button.
7. When the program is completed, turn the Outer Bowl and release it from the machine.
8. Transfer the shake into serving glasses and serve immediately.

Nutrition Info:

- InfoCalories: 142,Fat: 5.9g,Carbohydrates: 20.8g,Protein: 2.2.

Gelato Recipes

Red Velvet Gelato

Servings:4
Cooking Time:x
Ingredients:

- 4 large egg yolks
- ¼ cup granulated sugar
- 2 tablespoons unsweetened cocoa powder
- 1 cup whole milk
- ⅓ cup heavy (whipping) cream
- ¼ cup cream cheese, at room temperature
- 1 teaspoon vanilla extract
- 1 teaspoon red food coloring

Directions:

1. Fill a large bowl with ice water and set it aside.
2. In a small saucepan, whisk together the egg yolks, sugar, and cocoa powder until everything is fully combined and the sugar is dissolved. Do not do this over heat.
3. Whisk in the milk, heavy cream, cream cheese, vanilla, and food coloring.
4. Place the pan over medium heat. Cook, stirring constantly with a rubber spatula, until the temperature reaches 165°F to 175°F on an instant-read thermometer.
5. Remove the pan from the heat and pour the base through a fine-mesh strainer into a clean CREAMi Pint. Carefully place the container in the prepared ice water bath, making sure the water doesn't spill into the base.
6. Once the base has cooled, place the storage lid on the pint and freeze for 24 hours.
7. Remove the pint from the freezer and take off the lid. Place the pint in the outer bowl of your Ninja CREAMi, install the Creamerizer Paddle in the outer bowl lid, and lock the lid assembly onto the outer bowl. Place the bowl assembly on the motor base, and twist the handle to the right to raise the platform and lock it in place. Select the Gelato function.
8. Once the machine has finished processing, remove the gelato from the pint. Serve immediately.

Spirulina Cookie Gelato

Servings: 4
Cooking Time: 3 Minutes
Ingredients:

- 4 large egg yolks
- 1/3 C. granulated sugar
- 1 C. oat milk
- 1 tsp. vanilla extract
- 1 tsp. blue spirulina powder
- 4 small crunchy chocolate chip cookies, crumbled

Directions:

1. In a small saucepan, add the egg yolks and sugar and beat until well combined.
2. Add oat milk and vanilla extract and stir to combine.
3. Place the saucepan over medium heat and cook for about 2-3 minutes, stirring continuously.
4. Remove from the heat and through a fine-mesh strainer, strain the mixture into an empty Ninja CREAMi pint container.
5. Place the container into an ice bath to cool.
6. After cooling, cover the container with the storage lid and freeze for 24 hours.
7. After 24 hours, remove the lid from container and arrange into the outer bowl of Ninja CREAMi.
8. Install the "Creamerizer Paddle" onto the lid of outer bowl.
9. Then rotate the lid clockwise to lock.
10. Press "Power" button to turn on the unit.
11. Then press "GELATO" button.
12. When the program is completed, with a spoon, create a 1½-inch wide hole in the center that reaches the bottom of the pint container.
13. Add the chocolate chip cookies into the hole and press "MIX-IN" button.
14. When the program is completed, turn the outer bowl and release it from the machine.
15. Transfer the gelato into serving bowls and serve immediately.

Nutrition Info:

- InfoCalories: 235,Carbohydrates: 35.4g,Protein: 4.5g,Fat: 8.9g,Sodium: 104m.

Sweet Potato Gelato

Servings: 4
Cooking Time: 3 Minutes
Ingredients:

- ½ C. canned sweet potato puree
- 4 large egg yolks
- ¼ C. sugar
- ½ tsp. ground cinnamon
- 1/8 tsp. ground nutmeg
- 1 C. heavy cream
- 1 tsp. vanilla extract

Directions:

1. In a small saucepan, add the sweet potato puree, egg yolks, sugar, ½ tsp. of cinnamon and nutmeg and beat until well combined.
2. Add the heavy cream and vanilla extract and beat until well combined.
3. Place the saucepan over medium heat and cook for about 2-3 minutes, stirring continuously.
4. Remove from the heat and through a fine-mesh strainer, strain the mixture into an empty Ninja CREAMi pint container.
5. Place the container into an ice bath to cool.
6. After cooling, cover the container with the storage lid and freeze for 24 hours.
7. After 24 hours, remove the lid from container and arrange into the outer bowl of Ninja CREAMi.
8. Install the "Creamerizer Paddle" onto the lid of outer bowl.
9. Then rotate the lid clockwise to lock.
10. Press "Power" button to turn on the unit.
11. Then press "GELATO" button.
12. When the program is completed, turn the outer bowl and release it from the machine.
13. Transfer the gelato into serving bowls and serve immediately.

Nutrition Info:

- InfoCalories: 239,Carbohydrates: 21.5g,Protein: 4g,Fat: 15.7g,Sodium: 44m.

Caramel Egg Gelato

Servings: 4
Cooking Time: 10 Minutes
Ingredients:

- ¼ C. agave nectar
- ¾ C. unsweetened soy milk
- ½ C. unsweetened creamer
- 2 eggs
- 3 tbsp. granulated sugar
- ¼ C. caramels, chopped

Directions:

1. In a medium saucepan, add agave nectar over medium-high heat and cook for about 2-3 minutes.
2. Remove the saucepan from heat and slowly whisk in the soy milk and creamer.
3. Return the pan over medium-high heat and whisk in the eggs and sugar.
4. Cook for about 4-5 minutes, stirring frequently.
5. Remove from the heat and through a fine-mesh strainer, strain the mixture into an empty Ninja CREAMi pint container.
6. Place the container into an ice bath to cool.
7. After cooling, cover the container with the storage lid and freeze for 24 hours.
8. After 24 hours, remove the lid from container and arrange into the outer bowl of Ninja CREAMi.
9. Install the "Creamerizer Paddle" onto the lid of outer bowl.
10. Then rotate the lid clockwise to lock.
11. Press "Power" button to turn on the unit.
12. Then press "GELATO" button.
13. When the program is completed, with a spoon, create a 1½-inch wide hole in the center that reaches the bottom of the pint container.
14. Add the chopped caramels into the hole and press "MIX-IN" button.
15. When the program is completed, turn the outer bowl and release it from the machine.
16. Transfer the gelato into serving bowls and serve immediately.

Nutrition Info:

- InfoCalories: 174,Carbohydrates: 29.8g,Protein: 4.6g,Fat: 4.8g,Sodium: 66m.

Banana & Squash Cookie Gelato

Servings: 4
Cooking Time: 3 Minutes
Ingredients:

- 4 large egg yolks
- 1 C. heavy cream
- 1/3 C. granulated sugar
- ½ of banana, peeled and sliced
- ½ C. frozen butternut squash, chopped
- 1 box instant vanilla pudding mix
- 6 vanilla wafer cookies, crumbled

Directions:

1. In a small saucepan, add the egg yolks, heavy cream and sugar and beat until well combined.
2. Place the saucepan over medium heat and cook for about 2-3 minutes, stirring continuously.
3. Remove from the heat and through a fine-mesh strainer, strain the mixture into an empty Ninja CREAMi pint container.
4. Place the container into an ice bath to cool.
5. After cooling, add in the banana, squash and pudding until well combined.
6. Cover the container with the storage lid and freeze for 24 hours.
7. After 24 hours, remove the lid from container and arrange into the outer bowl of Ninja CREAMi.
8. Install the "Creamerizer Paddle" onto the lid of outer bowl.
9. Then rotate the lid clockwise to lock.
10. Press "Power" button to turn on the unit.
11. Then press "GELATO" button.
12. When the program is completed, with a spoon, create a 1½-inch wide hole in the center that reaches the bottom of the pint container.
13. Add the wafer cookies into the hole and press "MIX-IN" button.
14. When the program is completed, turn the outer bowl and release it from the machine.
15. Transfer the gelato into serving bowls and serve immediately.

Nutrition Info:

- InfoCalories: 489,Carbohydrates: 61.6g,Protein: 5.7g,Fat: 24.7g,Sodium: 194m.

Chocolate Hazelnut Gelato

Servings: 4
Cooking Time: 3 Minutes
Ingredients:

- 3 large egg yolks
- 1/3 C. hazelnut spread
- ¼ C. granulated sugar
- 2 tsp. cocoa powder
- 1 tbsp. light corn syrup
- 1 C. whole milk
- ½ C. heavy cream
- 1 tsp. vanilla extract

Directions:

1. In a small saucepan, add the egg yolks, hazelnut spread, sugar, cocoa powder and corn syrup and beat until well combined.
2. Add the milk, heavy cream and vanilla extract and beat until well combined.
3. Place the saucepan over medium heat and cook for about 2-3 minutes, stirring continuously.
4. Remove from the heat and through a fine-mesh strainer, strain the mixture into an empty Ninja CREAMi pint container.
5. Place the container into an ice bath to cool.
6. After cooling, cover the container with the storage lid and freeze for 24 hours.
7. After 24 hours, remove the lid from container and arrange into the outer bowl of Ninja CREAMi.
8. Install the "Creamerizer Paddle" onto the lid of outer bowl.
9. Then rotate the lid clockwise to lock.
10. Press "Power" button to turn on the unit.
11. Then press "GELATO" button.
12. When the program is completed, turn the outer bowl and release it from the machine.
13. Transfer the gelato into serving bowls and serve immediately.

Nutrition Info:

- InfoCalories: 321,Carbohydrates: 33.7g,Protein: 5.9g,Fat: 19g,Sodium: 50m.

Pistachio Gelato

Servings:4
Cooking Time:x
Ingredients:

- 4 large egg yolks
- ¼ cup plus 1 tablespoon granulated sugar
- 1 tablespoon light corn syrup
- ⅓ cup whole milk
- 1 cup heavy (whipping) cream
- 1 teaspoon almond extract
- 5 drops green food coloring
- ¼ cup roasted pistachios

Directions:
1. Fill a large bowl with ice water and set it aside.
2. In a small saucepan, whisk together the egg yolks, sugar, and corn syrup until the mixture is fully combined and the sugar is dissolved. Do not do this over heat.
3. Whisk in the milk, heavy cream, almond extract, and food coloring.
4. Place the pan over medium heat. Cook, stirring constantly with a rubber spatula, until the temperature reaches 165°F to 175°F on an instant-read thermometer.
5. Remove the pan from the heat and pour the base through a fine-mesh strainer into a clean CREAMi Pint. Carefully place the container in the prepared ice water bath, making sure the water doesn't spill into the base.
6. Once the base has cooled, place the storage lid on the pint and freeze for 24 hours.
7. Remove the pint from the freezer and take off the lid. Place the pint in the outer bowl of your Ninja CREAMi, install the Creamerizer Paddle in the outer bowl lid, and lock the lid assembly onto the outer bowl. Place the bowl assembly on the motor base, and twist the handle to the right to raise the platform and lock it in place. Select the Gelato function.
8. Once the machine has finished processing, remove the lid from the pint container. With a spoon, create a 1½-inch-wide hole that reaches the bottom of the pint. During this process, it is okay if your treat reaches above the Max Fill line. Add the pistachios to the hole in the pint, replace the lid, and select the Mix-In function.
9. Once the machine has finished processing, remove the gelato from the pint. Serve immediately.

Carrot Gelato

Servings: 4
Cooking Time: 3 Minutes
Ingredients:

- 3 large egg yolks
- 1/3 C. coconut sugar
- 1 tbsp. brown rice syrup
- ½ C. heavy cream
- 1 C. unsweetened almond milk
- ½ C. carrot puree
- ½ tsp. ground cinnamon
- ¼ tsp. ground nutmeg
- ¼ tsp. ground ginger
- ¼ tsp. ground cloves
- ¾ tsp. vanilla extract

Directions:
1. In a small saucepan, add the egg yolks, coconut sugar and brown rice syrup and beat until well combined.
2. Add the heavy cream, almond milk, carrot puree and spices and beat until well combined.
3. Place the saucepan over medium heat and cook for about 2-3 minutes, stirring continuously.
4. Remove from the heat and stir in the vanilla extract.
5. Through a fine-mesh strainer, strain the mixture into an empty Ninja CREAMi pint container.
6. Place the container into an ice bath to cool.
7. After cooling, cover the container with the storage lid and freeze for 24 hours.
8. After 24 hours, remove the lid from container and arrange into the outer bowl of Ninja CREAMi.
9. Install the "Creamerizer Paddle" onto the lid of outer bowl.
10. Then rotate the lid clockwise to lock.
11. Press "Power" button to turn on the unit.
12. Then press "GELATO" button.
13. When the program is completed, turn the outer bowl and release it from the machine.
14. Transfer the gelato into serving bowls and serve immediately.

Nutrition Info:
- InfoCalories: 146,Carbohydrates: 22.7g,Protein: 0.8g,Fat: 6.5g,Sodium: 64m.

Apple Cider Sorbet

Servings:4
Cooking Time:x
Ingredients:
- 1 cup apple cider
- 1 cup applesauce
- 2 tablespoons organic sugar

Directions:
1. In a large bowl, whisk together the apple cider, applesauce, and sugar until the sugar is dissolved.
2. Pour the base into a clean CREAMi Pint. Place the storage lid on the container and freeze for 24 hours.
3. Remove the pint from the freezer and take off the lid. Place the pint in the outer bowl of your Ninja CREAMi, install the Creamerizer Paddle in the outer bowl lid, and lock the lid assembly onto the outer bowl. Place the bowl assembly on the motor base, and twist the handle to the right to raise the platform and lock it in place. Select the Sorbet function.
4. Once the machine has finished processing, remove the sorbet from the pint. Serve immediately.

Vanilla Gelato

Servings: 4
Cooking Time: 3 Minutes
Ingredients:
- 4 large egg yolks
- 1 tbsp. light corn syrup
- ¼ C. plus 1 tbsp. granulated sugar
- 1 C. heavy cream
- 1/3 C. whole milk
- 1 whole vanilla bean, split in half lengthwise and scraped

Directions:
1. In a small saucepan, add the egg yolks, corn syrup and sugar and beat until well combined.
2. Add the heavy cream, milk and vanilla bean and beat until well combined.
3. Place the saucepan over medium heat and cook for about 2-3 minutes, stirring continuously.
4. Remove from the heat and through a fine-mesh strainer, strain the mixture into an empty Ninja CREAMi pint container.
5. Place the container into an ice bath to cool.
6. After cooling, cover the container with the storage lid and freeze for 24 hours.
7. After 24 hours, remove the lid from container and arrange into the outer bowl of Ninja CREAMi.
8. Install the "Creamerizer Paddle" onto the lid of outer bowl.
9. Then rotate the lid clockwise to lock.
10. Press "Power" button to turn on the unit.
11. Then press "GELATO" button.
12. When the program is completed, turn the outer bowl and release it from the machine.
13. Transfer the gelato into serving bowls and serve immediately.

Nutrition Info:
- InfoCalories: 239,Carbohydrates: 21g,Protein: 4g,Fat: 16.3g,Sodium: 28m.

Triple Chocolate Gelato

Servings: 4
Cooking Time: 3 Minutes
Ingredients:

- 4 large egg yolks
- 1/3 C. dark brown sugar
- 2 tbsp. dark cocoa powder
- 1 tbsp. chocolate fudge topping
- ¾ C. heavy cream
- ¾ C. whole milk
- 2-3 tbsp. chocolate chunks, chopped

Directions:

1. In a small saucepan, add the egg yolks, sugar, cocoa powder and chocolate fudge and beat until well combined.
2. Add the heavy cream and milk and beat until well combined.
3. Place the saucepan over medium heat and cook for about 2-3 minutes, stirring continuously.
4. Remove from the heat and stir in chocolate chunks until melted completely.
5. Through a fine-mesh strainer, strain the mixture into an empty Ninja CREAMi pint container.
6. Place the container into an ice bath to cool.
7. After cooling, cover the container with the storage lid and freeze for 24 hours.
8. After 24 hours, remove the lid from container and arrange into the outer bowl of Ninja CREAMi.
9. Install the "Creamerizer Paddle" onto the lid of outer bowl.
10. Then rotate the lid clockwise to lock.
11. Press "Power" button to turn on the unit.
12. Then press "GELATO" button.
13. When the program is completed, turn the outer bowl and release it from the machine.
14. Transfer the gelato into serving bowls and serve immediately.

Nutrition Info:

- InfoCalories: 256,Carbohydrates: 22.8g,Protein: 5.8g,Fat: 16.7g,Sodium: 59m.

Peanut Butter Gelato

Servings: 4
Cooking Time: 10 Minutes
Ingredients:

- 1½ C. unsweetened coconut milk
- 6 tbsp. sugar
- 1 tbsp. cornstarch
- 3 tbsp. peanut butter
- 3 dark chocolate peanut butter C., cut each into 8 pieces
- 2 tbsp. peanuts, chopped

Directions:

1. In a small saucepan, add the coconut milk, sugar, and cornstarch and mix well.
2. Place the saucepan over medium heat and bring to a boil, beating continuously.
3. Reduce the heat to low and simmer for about 3-4 minutes.
4. Remove from the heat and stir in the peanut butter.
5. Transfer the mixture into an empty Ninja CREAMi pint container.
6. Place the container into an ice bath to cool.
7. After cooling, cover the container with the storage lid and freeze for 24 hours.
8. After 24 hours, remove the lid from container and arrange into the outer bowl of Ninja CREAMi.
9. Install the "Creamerizer Paddle" onto the lid of outer bowl.
10. Then rotate the lid clockwise to lock.
11. Press "Power" button to turn on the unit.
12. Then press "GELATO" button.
13. When the program is completed, with a spoon, create a 1½-inch wide hole in the center that reaches the bottom of the pint container.
14. Add the peanut butter C. and peanuts into the hole and press "MIX-IN" button.
15. When the program is completed, turn the outer bowl and release it from the machine.
16. Transfer the gelato into serving bowls and serve immediately.

Nutrition Info:

- InfoCalories: 426,Carbohydrates: 34.2g,Protein: 6.8g,Fat: 29.7g,Sodium: 124m.

Tiramisu Gelato

Servings:4
Cooking Time:x
Ingredients:
- 4 large egg yolks
- ⅓ cup granulated sugar
- 1 cup whole milk
- ⅓ cup heavy (whipping) cream
- ¼ cup cream cheese
- 1 tablespoon instant coffee
- 1 teaspoon rum extract
- ¼ cup ladyfinger pieces

Directions:
1. Fill a large bowl with ice water and set it aside.
2. In a small saucepan, whisk together the egg yolks and sugar until the mixture is fully combined and the sugar is dissolved. Do not do this over heat.
3. Whisk in the milk, heavy cream, cream cheese, instant coffee, and rum extract.
4. Place the pan over medium heat. Cook, stirring constantly with a rubber spatula, until the temperature reaches 165°F to 175°F on an instant-read thermometer.
5. Remove the pan from the heat and pour the base through a fine-mesh strainer into a clean CREAMi Pint. Carefully place the container in the prepared ice water bath, making sure the water doesn't spill into the base.
6. Once the base has cooled, place the storage lid on the pint and freeze for 24 hours.
7. Remove the pint from the freezer and take off the lid. Place the pint in the outer bowl of your Ninja CREAMi, install the Creamerizer Paddle in the outer bowl lid, and lock the lid assembly onto the outer bowl. Place the bowl assembly on the motor base, and twist the handle to the right to raise the platform and lock it in place. Select the Gelato function.
8. Once the machine has finished processing, remove the lid from the pint container. With a spoon, create a 1½-inch-wide hole that reaches the bottom of the pint. During this process, it is okay if your treat reaches above the Max Fill line. Add the ladyfinger pieces to the hole in the pint, replace the lid, and select the Mix-In function.
9. Once the machine has finished processing, remove the gelato from the pint. Serve immediately.

Orange Sherbet

Servings:4
Cooking Time:x
Ingredients:
- 1 cup orange juice
- ¼ cup plus 1 tablespoon granulated sugar
- ¼ cup whole milk
- ½ cup heavy (whipping) cream

Directions:
1. In a large bowl, whisk together the orange juice, sugar, milk, and heavy cream until everything is well combined and the sugar is dissolved.
2. Pour the base into a clean CREAMi Pint. Place the storage lid on the container and freeze for 24 hours.
3. Remove the pint from the freezer and take off the lid. Place the pint in the outer bowl of your Ninja CREAMi, install the Creamerizer Paddle in the outer bowl lid, and lock the lid assembly onto the outer bowl. Place the bowl assembly on the motor base, and twist the handle to the right to raise the platform and lock it in place. Select the Ice Cream function.
4. Once the machine has finished processing, remove the sherbet from the pint. Serve immediately with desired toppings.

Strawberry Cheesecake Gelato

Servings:4
Cooking Time:x

Ingredients:

- NUT-FREE, FAMILY FAVORITE
- PREP TIME: 5 minutes / Cook time: 7 to 10 minutes / Freeze time: 24 hours
- FUNCTIONS: Gelato and Mix-In
- TOOLS NEEDED: Large bowl, small saucepan, whisk, rubber spatula, instant-read thermometer, fine-mesh strainer, spoon
- 4 large egg yolks
- 3 tablespoons granulated sugar
- 1 cup whole milk
- ⅓ cup heavy (whipping) cream
- ¼ cup cream cheese, at room temperature
- 1 teaspoon vanilla extract
- 3 tablespoons strawberry jam
- ¼ cup graham cracker pieces

Directions:

1. Fill a large bowl with ice water and set it aside.
2. In a small saucepan, whisk together the egg yolks and sugar until the mixture is smooth and the sugar is dissolved. Do not do this over heat.
3. Whisk in the milk, heavy cream, cream cheese, vanilla, and strawberry jam.
4. Place the pan over medium heat. Cook, stirring constantly with a rubber spatula, until the temperature reaches 165°F to 175°F on an instant-read thermometer.
5. Remove the pan from the heat and pour the base through a fine-mesh strainer into a clean CREAMi Pint. Carefully place the container in the prepared ice water bath, making sure the water doesn't spill into the base.
6. Once the base has cooled, place the storage lid on the pint and freeze for 24 hours.
7. Remove the pint from the freezer and take off the lid. Place the pint in the outer bowl of your Ninja CREAMi, install the Creamerizer Paddle in the outer bowl lid, and lock the lid assembly onto the outer bowl. Place the bowl assembly on the motor base, and twist the handle to the right to raise the platform and lock it in place. Select the Gelato function.
8. Once the machine has finished processing, remove the lid from the pint container. With a spoon, create a 1½-inch-wide hole that reaches the bottom of the pint. During this process, it is okay if your treat reaches above the Max Fill line. Add the graham cracker pieces to the hole in the pint, replace the lid, and select the Mix-In function.
9. Once the machine has finished processing, remove the gelato from the pint. Serve immediately.

Chocolate-hazelnut Gelato

Servings:4
Cooking Time:x
Ingredients:

- 3 large egg yolks
- ⅓ cup chocolate-hazelnut spread
- 2 teaspoons unsweetened cocoa powder
- 1 tablespoon corn syrup
- ¼ cup granulated sugar
- 1 cup whole milk
- ½ cup heavy (whipping) cream
- 1 teaspoon vanilla extract

Directions:

1. Fill a large bowl with ice water and set it aside.
2. In a small saucepan, whisk together the egg yolks, chocolate-hazelnut spread, cocoa powder, corn syrup, and sugar until the mixture is fully combined and the sugar is dissolved. Do not do this over heat.
3. Whisk in the milk, heavy cream, and vanilla.
4. Place the pan over medium heat. Cook, stirring constantly with a rubber spatula, until the temperature reaches 165°F to 175°F on an instant-read thermometer.
5. Remove the pan from the heat and pour the base through a fine-mesh strainer into a clean CREAMi Pint. Carefully place the container in the prepared ice water bath, making sure the water doesn't spill into the base.
6. Once the base has cooled, place the storage lid on the pint and freeze for 24 hours.
7. Remove the pint from the freezer and take off the lid. Place the pint in the outer bowl of your Ninja CREAMi, install the Creamerizer Paddle in the outer bowl lid, and lock the lid assembly onto the outer bowl. Place the bowl assembly on the motor base, and twist the handle to the right to raise the platform and lock it in place. Select the Gelato function.
8. Once the machine has finished processing, remove the gelato from the pint. Serve immediately with desired toppings.

Marshmallow Cookie Gelato

Servings: 4
Cooking Time: 6 Minutes
Ingredients:

- 1 whole vanilla bean, split in half lengthwise, scraped
- 4 egg yolks
- ¾ C. heavy cream
- 1/3 C. whole milk
- 2 tbsp. granulated sugar
- 1 tbsp. light corn syrup
- 1 tsp. vanilla extract
- 5 tbsp. marshmallow paste
- 5 peanut butter cookies, chopped

Directions:

1. In a medium saucepan, add the vanilla bean over medium-high heat, and toast for about 2-3 minutes, stirring continuously.
2. Reduce the heat to medium-low and whisk in the egg yolks, heavy cream, milk, sugar, corn syrup and vanilla extract.
3. Cook for about 2-3 minutes, stirring continuously.
4. Remove from the heat and through a fine-mesh strainer, strain the mixture into an empty Ninja CREAMi pint container.
5. Place the container into an ice bath to cool.
6. After cooling, cover the container with the storage lid and freeze for 24 hours.
7. After 24 hours, remove the lid from container and arrange into the outer bowl of Ninja CREAMi.
8. Install the "Creamerizer Paddle" onto the lid of outer bowl.
9. Then rotate the lid clockwise to lock.
10. Press "Power" button to turn on the unit.
11. Then press "GELATO" button.
12. When the program is completed, with a spoon, create a 1½-inch wide hole in the center that reaches the bottom of the pint container.
13. Add the cookies into the hole and press "MIX-IN" button.
14. When the program is completed, turn the outer bowl and release it from the machine.
15. Transfer the gelato into serving bowls and serve immediately.

Nutrition Info:

- InfoCalories: 345,Carbohydrates: 31.9g,Protein: 6.3g,Fat: 21g,Sodium: 103m.

Berries Mascarpone Gelato

Servings: 4
Cooking Time: 3 Minutes
Ingredients:

- 3 large egg yolks
- ½ C. plus 2 tbsp. granulated sugar, divided
- 1 tbsp. light corn syrup
- ½ C. mascarpone
- ¾ C. whole milk
- ¼ C. heavy cream
- ½ tsp. vanilla extract
- 1 C. frozen mixed berries

Directions:

1. In a small saucepan, add the egg yolks, ½ C. of sugar and corn syrup and beat until well combined.
2. Add the mascarpone milk, heavy cream and vanilla extract and beat until well combined.
3. Place the saucepan over medium heat and cook for about 2-3 minutes, stirring continuously.
4. Remove from the heat and through a fine-mesh strainer, strain the mixture into an empty Ninja CREAMi pint container.
5. Place the container into an ice bath to cool.
6. After cooling, cover the container with the storage lid and freeze for 24 hours.
7. Meanwhile, in a small saucepan, add the mixed berries and remaining sugar over medium heat and cook for about 8 minutes, stirring occasionally and mashing to form a thick jam.
8. Remove from heat and transfer the jam into a bowl.
9. Refrigerate the jam until using.
10. After 24 hours, remove the lid from container and arrange the container into the outer bowl of Ninja CREAMi.
11. Install the "Creamerizer Paddle" onto the lid of outer bowl.
12. Then rotate the lid clockwise to lock.
13. Press "Power" button to turn on the unit.
14. Then press "GELATO" button.
15. When the program is completed, with a spoon, create a 1½-inch wide hole in the center that reaches the bottom of the pint container.
16. Add the berry jam into the hole and press "MIX-IN" button.
17. When the program is completed, turn the outer bowl and release it from the machine.
18. Transfer the gelato into serving bowls and serve immediately.

Nutrition Info:

- InfoCalories: 295,Carbohydrates: 41.6g,Protein: 7.4g,Fat: 11.8g,Sodium: 54m.

Maple Gelato

Servings: 4
Cooking Time: 3 Minutes
Ingredients:

- 4 large egg yolks
- ½ C. plus 1 tbsp. light brown sugar
- 1 tbsp. maple syrup
- 1 tsp. maple extract
- 1 C. whole milk
- 1/3 C. heavy cream

Directions:

1. In a small saucepan, add the egg yolks, brown sugar, maple syrup and maple extract and beat until well combined.
2. Add the milk and heavy cream and beat until well combined.
3. Place the saucepan over medium heat and cook for about 2-3 minutes, stirring continuously.
4. Remove from the heat and through a fine-mesh strainer, strain the mixture into an empty Ninja CREAMi pint container.
5. Place the container into an ice bath to cool.
6. After cooling, cover the container with the storage lid and freeze for 24 hours.
7. After 24 hours, remove the lid from container and arrange into the outer bowl of Ninja CREAMi.
8. Install the "Creamerizer Paddle" onto the lid of outer bowl.
9. Then rotate the lid clockwise to lock.
10. Press "Power" button to turn on the unit.
11. Then press "GELATO" button.
12. When the program is completed, turn the outer bowl and release it from the machine.
13. Transfer the gelato into serving bowls and serve immediately.

Nutrition Info:

- InfoCalories: 218,Carbohydrates: 27g,Protein: 4.9g,Fat: 10.2g,Sodium: 43m.

Pumpkin Gelato

Servings: 4
Cooking Time: 3 Minutes
Ingredients:

- 3 large egg yolks
- 1/3 C. granulated sugar
- 1 tbsp. light corn syrup
- 1 C. whole milk
- ½ C. heavy cream
- ½ C. canned pumpkin puree
- 1½ tsp. pumpkin pie spice
- 1 tsp. vanilla extract

Directions:

1. In a small saucepan, add the egg yolks, sugar and corn syrup and beat until well combined.
2. Add the milk, heavy cream, pumpkin puree and pumpkin pie spice and beat until well combined.
3. Place the saucepan over medium heat and cook for about 2-3 minutes, stirring continuously.
4. Remove from the heat and stir in the vanilla extract.
5. Through a fine-mesh strainer, strain the mixture into an empty Ninja CREAMi pint container.
6. Place the container into an ice bath to cool.
7. After cooling, cover the container with the storage lid and freeze for 24 hours.
8. After 24 hours, remove the lid from container and arrange into the outer bowl of Ninja CREAMi.
9. Install the "Creamerizer Paddle" onto the lid of outer bowl.
10. Then rotate the lid clockwise to lock.
11. Press "Power" button to turn on the unit.
12. Then press "GELATO" button.
13. When the program is completed, turn the outer bowl and release it from the machine.
14. Transfer the gelato into serving bowls and serve immediately.

Nutrition Info:

- InfoCalories: 220,Carbohydrates: 27g,Protein: 4.7g,Fat: 11.1g,Sodium: 39m.

Vanilla Bean Gelato

Servings:4
Cooking Time:x
Ingredients:

- 4 large egg yolks
- 1 tablespoon light corn syrup
- ¼ cup plus 1 tablespoon granulated sugar
- ⅓ cup whole milk
- 1 cup heavy (whipping) cream
- 1 whole vanilla bean, split in half lengthwise and scraped

Directions:

1. Fill a large bowl with ice water and set it aside.
2. In a small saucepan, whisk together the egg yolks, corn syrup, and sugar until everything is fully combined and the sugar is dissolved. Do not do this over heat.
3. Whisk in the milk, heavy cream, and vanilla bean scrapings (discard the pod).
4. Place the pan over medium heat. Cook, stirring constantly with a rubber spatula, until the temperature reaches 165°F to 175°F on an instant-read thermometer.
5. Remove the pan from the heat and pour the base through a fine-mesh strainer into a clean CREAMi Pint. Carefully place the container in the prepared ice water bath, making sure the water doesn't spill into the base.
6. Once the base has cooled, place the storage lid on the pint and freeze for 24 hours.
7. Remove the pint from the freezer and take off the lid. Place the pint in the outer bowl of your Ninja CREAMi, install the Creamerizer Paddle in the outer bowl lid, and lock the lid assembly onto the outer bowl. Place the bowl assembly on the motor base, and twist the handle to the right to raise the platform and lock it in place. Select the Gelato function.
8. Once the machine has finished processing, remove the gelato from the pint. Serve immediately with desired toppings.

Marshmallow Gelato

Servings: 4
Cooking Time: 5 Minutes

Ingredients:

- 1 C. whole milk
- ½ C. heavy cream
- ¼ C. sugar
- 3 egg yolk
- Pinch of sea salt
- ¼ C. mini marshmallows

Directions:

1. Preheat the oven to broiler. Lightly grease a baking sheet.
2. Arrange the marshmallows onto the prepared baking sheet in a single layer.
3. Broil for about 5 minutes, flipping once halfway through.
4. Meanwhile, in a small saucepan, add the milk, heavy cream, sugar, egg yolks and a pinch of salt and beat until well combined.
5. Place the saucepan over medium heat and cook for about 1 minute, stirring continuously.
6. Remove from the heat and stir in half of the marshmallows.
7. Transfer the mixture into an empty Ninja CREAMi pint container.
8. Place the container into an ice bath to cool.
9. After cooling, cover the container with the storage lid and freeze for 24 hours.
10. Reserve the remaining marshmallows into the freezer.
11. After 24 hours, remove the lid from container and arrange into the outer bowl of Ninja CREAMi.
12. Install the "Creamerizer Paddle" onto the lid of outer bowl.
13. Then rotate the lid clockwise to lock.
14. Press "Power" button to turn on the unit.
15. Then press "GELATO" button.
16. When the program is completed, with a spoon, create a 1½-inch wide hole in the center that reaches the bottom of the pint container.
17. Add the reserved frozen marshmallows into the hole and press "MIX-IN" button.
18. When the program is completed, turn the outer bowl and release it from the machine.
19. Transfer the gelato into serving bowls and serve immediately.

Nutrition Info:

- InfoCalories: 186,Carbohydrates: 18.7g,Protein: 4.4g,Fat: 10.9g,Sodium: 77m.

Blueberry & Crackers Gelato

Servings: 4
Cooking Time: 3 Minutes

Ingredients:

- 4 large egg yolks
- 3 tbsp. granulated sugar
- 3 tbsp. wild blueberry preserves
- 1 tsp. vanilla extract
- 1 C. whole milk
- 1/3 C. heavy cream
- ¼ C. cream cheese, softened
- 3-6 drops purple food coloring
- 2 large graham crackers, broken in 1-inch pieces

Directions:

1. In a small saucepan, add the egg yolks, sugar, blueberry preserves and vanilla extract and beat until well combined.
2. Add the milk, heavy cream, cream cheese and food coloring and beat until well combined.
3. Place the saucepan over medium heat and cook for about 2-3 minutes, stirring continuously.
4. Remove from the heat and through a fine-mesh strainer, strain the mixture into an empty Ninja CREAMi pint container.
5. Place the container into an ice bath to cool.
6. After cooling, cover the container with the storage lid and freeze for 24 hours.
7. After 24 hours, remove the lid from container and arrange into the outer bowl of Ninja CREAMi.
8. Install the "Creamerizer Paddle" onto the lid of outer bowl.
9. Then rotate the lid clockwise to lock.
10. Press "Power" button to turn on the unit.
11. Then press "GELATO" button.
12. When the program is completed, with a spoon, create a 1½-inch wide hole in the center that reaches the bottom of the pint container.
13. Add the graham crackers into the hole and press "MIX-IN" button.
14. When the program is completed, turn the outer bowl and release it from the machine.
15. Transfer the gelato into serving bowls and serve immediately.

Nutrition Info:

- InfoCalories: 279,Carbohydrates: 28.3g,Protein: 6.4g,Fat: 16g,Sodium: 122m.

White Chocolate–raspberry Gelato

Servings:4
Cooking Time:x
Ingredients:

- 1 cup whole milk, divided
- 1 tablespoon, plus ¼ cup cornstarch
- ½ cup heavy (whipping) cream
- 1 teaspoon vanilla extract
- ⅓ cup, plus ¾ cup granulated sugar
- ½ cup raspberries
- 4 tablespoons water, divided
- ¼ cup white chocolate chips

Directions:

1. Fill a large bowl with ice water and set it aside.
2. In a small bowl, mix together ⅓ cup of milk and 1 tablespoon of cornstarch; set aside.
3. In a small saucepan, combine the remaining ⅔ cup of milk, the heavy cream, vanilla, and ⅓ cup of sugar. Whisk thoroughly to combine.
4. Place the pan over medium-high heat and bring the mixture to a simmer for about 4 minutes. Whisk in the cornstarch slurry and continue whisking constantly for about 1 minute.
5. Remove the pan from the heat and pour the base through a fine-mesh strainer into a clean CREAMi Pint. Carefully place the container in the prepared ice water bath, making sure the water doesn't spill into the base.
6. While the base chills, place the raspberries, remaining ¾ cup of sugar, and 2 tablespoons of water in a small saucepan. Place the pan over medium heat. Cook, stirring constantly, for about 5 minutes, until the mixture is bubbling and the raspberries have broken down.
7. In a small bowl, whisk together the remaining 2 tablespoons of water and ¼ cup of cornstarch. Pour this mixture into the raspberry liquid. Continue to cook, stirring until the mixture has thickened, about 1 minute. Pour the raspberry mixture into a clean container, then carefully place the container in the ice water bath, making sure the water doesn't spill inside the container.
8. Once the base and raspberry mixtures are cold, carefully fold the raspberry mixture into the gelato base. Pour this mixture back into the CREAMi Pint, place the storage lid on the container, and freeze for 24 hours.
9. Remove the pint from the freezer and take off the lid. Place the pint in the outer bowl of your Ninja CREAMi, install the Creamerizer Paddle in the outer bowl lid, and lock the lid assembly onto the outer bowl. Place the bowl assembly on the motor base, and twist the handle to the right to raise the platform and lock it in place. Select the Gelato function.
10. Once the machine has finished processing, remove the lid from the pint. With a spoon, create a 1½-inch-wide hole that reaches the bottom of the pint. During this process, it is okay if your treat reaches above the Max Fill line. Add the white chocolate chips to the hole in the pint, replace the lid, and select the Mix-In function.
11. Once the machine has finished processing, remove the gelato from the pint. Serve immediately with desired toppings.

Squash Gelato

Servings: 4
Cooking Time: 5 Minutes
Ingredients:

- 1¾ C. milk
- ½ C. cooked butternut squash
- ¼ C. granulated sugar
- ½ tsp. ground cinnamon
- ¼ tsp. ground allspice
- Pinch of salt

Directions:

1. In a small saucepan, add all ingredients and beat until well combined.
2. Place the saucepan over medium heat and cook for about 5 minutes, stirring continuously.
3. Remove from the heat and transfer the mixture into an empty Ninja CREAMi pint container.
4. Place the container into an ice bath to cool.
5. After cooling, cover the container with the storage lid and freeze for 24 hours.
6. After 24 hours, remove the lid from container and arrange into the outer bowl of Ninja CREAMi.
7. Install the "Creamerizer Paddle" onto the lid of outer bowl.
8. Then rotate the lid clockwise to lock.
9. Press "Power" button to turn on the unit.
10. Then press "GELATO" button.
11. When the program is completed, turn the outer bowl and release it from the machine.
12. Transfer the gelato into serving bowls and serve immediately.

Nutrition Info:

- InfoCalories: 109,Carbohydrates: 20.1g,Protein: 3.7g,Fat: 2.2g,Sodium: 90m.

INDEX

Chocolate-covered Coconut And Almond Ice Cream 47
Chocolate-hazelnut Gelato 76
Chocolate-hazelnut Milkshake 67
Chocolate–peanut Butter Milkshake 64
Cinnamon Cereal Milk Ice Cream 52
Cinnamon Red Hot Ice Cream 21
Classic Vanilla Ice Cream 14
Coconut Ice Cream 16
Coconut Lime Sorbet 30
Coconut Mint Chip Ice Cream 57
Coffee And Cookies Ice Cream 49
Coffee Chip Ice Cream 54
Coffee Smoothie Bowl 37
Coffee Vodka Milkshake 65
Cookie Milkshake 61
Cookies & Cream Ice Cream 48
Cookies And Coconut Ice Cream 50

D

Dairy-free Strawberry Milkshake 62
Dulce De Leche Milkshake 59

E

Earl Grey Tea Ice Cream 16
Energy Elixir Smoothie 42

F

French Vanilla Ice Cream 21
Fruit Carrot Ice Cream 19
Fruity Carrot Ice Cream 22
Fruity Cereal Ice Cream 55
Fruity Coffee Smoothie Bowl 43

G

Gator Smoothies 44
Grape Sorbet 28
Grapes Sorbet 24
Grasshopper Ice Cream 56
Green Fruity Smoothie Bowl 45

H

Healthy Strawberry Shake 59

P

Papaya Smoothie Bowl 40
Peach Sorbet 34
Peanut Butter & Jelly Ice Cream 14
Peanut Butter Gelato 73
Pear Ice Cream 17
Pecan Milkshake 59
Piña Colada Smoothie Bowl 36
Pineapple & Dragon Fruit Smoothie Bowl 39
Pineapple Rum Sorbet 32
Pistachio Gelato 71
Pistachio Ice Cream 57
Plum Sorbet 32
Pomegranate & Blueberry Sorbet 25
Pumpkin & Banana Smoothie Bowl 42
Pumpkin Gelato 78
Pumpkin Smoothie Bowl 41

R

Raspberry Lime Sorbet 30
Raspberry Smoothie Bowl 43
Red Velvet Gelato 68
Rocky Road Ice Cream 54
Rum Raisin Ice Cream 50

S

Simple Smoothie Bowl 35
Snack Mix Ice Cream 48
Sneaky Mint Chip Ice Cream 46
Spirulina Cookie Gelato 68
Squash Gelato 81
Strawberries & Champagne Sorbet 27
Strawberry & Beet Sorbet 25
Strawberry & Kiwi Sorbet 31
Strawberry Cheesecake Gelato 75
Strawberry Ice Cream 12
Strawberry Smoothie Bowl 41
Strawberry Sorbet 23
Strawberry-carrot Ice Cream 11
Strawberry-orange Creme Smoothie 45
Super Lemon Ice Cream 20
Sweet Potato Gelato 69
Sweet Potato Pie Ice Cream 56

Made in United States
Troutdale, OR
05/03/2024

19616507R00051